GOD'S REALITY
SHOW

Starring eleven Old Testament housemates

MIKE COLES

Text copyright © Mike Coles 2005
The author asserts the moral right
to be identified as the author of this work

Published by
The Bible Reading Fellowship
First Floor, Elsfield Hall
15–17 Elsfield Way, Oxford OX2 8FG

ISBN 1 84101 367 6
First published 2005
10 9 8 7 6 5 4 3 2 1 0

Acknowledgments
Scripture quotations are based on the Good News Bible published by The Bible
Societies/HarperCollins Publishers Ltd, UK © American Bible Society 1966, 1971,
1976, 1992, used with permission.

A catalogue record for this book is available from the British Library

Printed and bound in Great Britain by
Bookmarque, Croydon

CONTENTS

INTRODUCTION

As if by some miracle, eleven Old Testament characters have suddenly all been brought together in one place. How this happened, we don't know. When it happened, we don't know. These questions aren't important. The fact is that these people have all been transported to a huge tent somewhere in the Judean wilderness.

When I say 'tent', I don't mean any old tent. This one is huge and pretty luxurious, the sort that was often erected to house the ark of the covenant (1 Chronicles 16:1). The tent is so big that there are actually quite a few different compartments inside. Just outside, there is a beautiful pool to bathe in, and next to this a well. More about the tent and living conditions later!

The Lord God has decided to get together eleven characters from the Old Testament. They are all to live together for seven days, and he will be watching them. He will set them little tasks, and every few days he will ask all the occupants in the tent to vote for one person to leave. They will have to give reasons for their vote. The winner of this experiment will be the last person, or maybe the last few, remaining. They won't actually win anything. Their prize is surviving to be the last remaining.

The interesting thing about the experiment is that some of the characters already know each other. Some have definitely heard about others (those that in 'real time' lived before them). At least one would not know anything about the others, as she is Eve, the first woman on earth, but all the others have definitely heard about her.

So, who are these characters that the Lord God has chosen? Let's look at the list, which is in order of who appears first in the Old Testament.

1. **Eve:** As far as dates are concerned, we'll say pre-history.
2. **Noah:** Again, we'll put him under pre-history.

3. **Joseph:** From 1800 to 1750BC.
4. **Moses:** For Moses we'll say about 1250–1210BC.
5. **Joshua:** Joshua led the first stage of the invasion into Canaan in about 1210BC.
6. **Rahab:** She, of course, is part of the Joshua story.
7. **Deborah:** One of the Judges, who lived about 1200–1050BC.
8. **Samson:** He was also one of the Judges (around 1200–1050BC).
9. **Ruth:** She lived during the times of the Judges (around 1200–1050BC).
10. **King Saul:** His reign was about 1030–1010BC.
11. **King David:** He ruled about 1010–970BC.

As you can see, a great bunch to get together, but how will they all get on? What will they have to talk about? How can Saul and David be put into the same house together? Won't Samson just smash the place up? Won't Eve simply get the blame for causing all the problems in the world? We will have to see what unfolds. Whatever happens, we'll come to learn a great deal about these characters and they'll be sharing stories of some of the many adventures they had in the course of their 'real time' lives.

Before we get started, we'll have a look at the set-up, what some of the rules are and so on. Then the characters will come into the tent one by one; the Lord God will introduce them to each other and tell them what it's all about.

As mentioned earlier, the eleven characters will be living together in a large tent, which has been erected in about two acres of land. Surrounding the tent is a huge wall, similar to the one that surrounded Jericho. It's about ten metres in height and two metres thick. There's no way that anyone will be leaving this tent! Samson may try smashing the wall down, Joshua may try walking around it seven times, but they won't succeed.

The eleven characters will arrive through a huge gate built into the wall. How they get there is not important. When they walk through the gate, the Lord God will speak to them and explain what is happening. They are all used to hearing the voice of the Lord, so they will listen and obey him. The characters will all be pretty much middle-aged in appearance, even though they have all lived their lives. Again how this happens is not our business. With the Lord, all things are possible! They will have no possessions with them. All the basic necessities, such as food and clothing, will be provided for them in the tent.

The characters will arrive in the order that they appear in the Old Testament, so Eve will arrive first, followed by Noah, Joseph, Moses and the others. They will be told that they will have to live together for seven days in the tent, within the mighty wall. The Lord God will explain that he will set them tasks to do, which, if completed successfully, will be rewarded, perhaps with extra food and wine. They will also learn that when the Lord God instructs them to do so, they will have to vote for one of the group to leave the tent through the large gate in the wall.

As they are men and women of God, we might hope that all the characters get on well, but will it be a total disaster? It's going to be fun to see how this little experiment is going to work! Let's move to that wilderness location and watch the characters arrive.

DAY ONE

The huge gate slowly opens and a woman dressed in animal skins walks through. It's Eve, probably wearing the same clothes that were made for her after the Fall.[1] We hear the Lord God's voice speaking to Eve.

'This is the Lord your God. I have brought you to this place. You are to wait here by the gate until I tell you what to do next. Wait in silence.'

Having disobeyed God once before, she isn't going to do so again. She stands in silence, looking totally confused.

A second figure appears at the gate. This time it's Noah—a well-built man, as you'd probably have to be to construct that huge ark. He is wearing some simple woven cloth garments. He immediately walks towards Eve, but before he has time to speak to her the voice of the Lord God addresses him.

'Noah, this is the Lord your God. I have brought you to this place. You may be confused, but all will be explained soon. You too must wait here in silence, until the others arrive, and then you will be introduced to each other.'

Eve and Noah look at each other but say nothing. They wait.

Joseph arrives—a handsome man, wearing an amazingly beautiful robe, long sleeved and woven with many different colours. It was quite unusual to see a garment like this in Joseph's time, as most people were ordinary workers on the land and clothes were simple and practical. A garment like this would take a long time to make and, with all the different coloured cloth, it would cost a fair bit. This is clearly the first thing that Noah and Eve notice as they both stand and stare at Joseph's awesome coat.

Again, before anyone can speak, the Lord God's voice booms out: 'Joseph, this is the Lord your God. I have brought you to this place. You are to wait here in silence with the others. All will be explained in time.'

The ever faithful and patient Joseph bows his head before the Lord. He waits with the others.

The three of them look towards the gate. Another man walks through. This man is a leader—there is something about him, some air of authority that draws the attention of the others. He walks towards them slowly yet majestically, holding some kind of stick or rod.[2]

'Moses,' says the Lord God. 'This is the Lord your God. Like the other three you see here, you have been brought here by me. You are not to speak to them or to me at the moment. Trust me. All will be revealed soon.'

Just as Joseph did before him, Moses bows his head in acknowledgment of what the Lord God has said to him. All of a sudden, though, he looks up towards the gate. The expression on his face is one of total amazement. Walking in at this moment is Joshua.

'Moses!' cries Joshua. 'What on earth is going on? Why are we here?' Before Moses can answer, the Lord God calls out. 'Silence! This is the Lord your God. I have brought you to this place. You are to wait for a few more to arrive. I will then reveal my plan to you all.'

Moses and Joshua hug each other silently, but their faces show that it's an emotional reunion. If the others were confused before, they are now totally baffled. They cannot understand why these two seem to know each other, or who they are. If the situation seemed confusing, the next guest doesn't help matters!

Rahab walks through the gate. Just as Joshua finishes hugging Moses, he catches sight of her and immediately runs over to embrace her. 'Rahab, it's wonderful to see you!'

'Joshua!' she says in a bewildered voice.

Moses looks as bemused as the others by now. Again the Lord God speaks. 'Welcome. This is the Lord your God who has brought you here. Wait in silence, and all will be explained.'

In walks Deborah, a fine-looking woman, tall and very upright. Like Moses, she looks to be a person of real authority. This time, there's no hugging, as clearly no one knows who she is. She receives the same welcome and explanation from the Lord as the others.

Everyone's jaw drops when the next guest arrives. 'Huge' is not the word! This man has muscles in places where most of us don't even have places. He also has jet-black, long, flowing hair. It's the mighty judge, Samson.

'What the hell's going on here?' Samson yells. The others take a step back. He's quite a frightening sight. Looking at him is scary enough, but hearing his voice at full blast because he's angry is terrifying.

'Silence!' thunders the voice of the Lord God. 'This is the Lord your God, who has brought you here. Wait in silence. I will explain all soon.'

'Why have you brought me here? Where is "here"?' Samson screams.

'Silence!' the Lord booms. 'You're still the wild one! When will you learn to obey me?'

Samson stands stock still, his mouth open in shock, clearly recalling some of the events of his life. The Lord is right: his life has been wild. He disobeys pretty much everything. He doesn't speak again, but waits like the others, who are still staring at him in disbelief. Not only is this man huge, but he dares to question the Lord.

They look towards the gate. Who on earth will turn up next?

This time it's Ruth the Moabite, wearing a simple blue robe and leather sandals. She's quite a small woman, with a calm, pretty face that suggests she might be fairly quiet, yet with some sort of inner strength. The Lord speaks to her as he did to the others.

A tall and very handsome man now walks through the gates. This is Saul, the first king of Israel. He looks at all the others, and you can imagine him saying to himself, 'I'm the king. Why aren't they bowing down to me?'

The Lord God speaks to him. 'Saul, this is the Lord your God.

You've disobeyed me many times. I give you one order now: wait with the others in silence. I will explain why you are here in a moment.'

The final guest arrives. It's David, the most famous king of Israel. As he walks through the gate, Saul's face turns purple and he bursts out furiously, 'No! I cannot be here with this man.' He dashes towards David and tries to grab him around the throat. Even though he is caught off-guard, David looks as if he could quite easily handle the situation himself, but Samson is already there. He picks Saul up with one hand and says, 'Listen here. The Lord God has given us an order. Pay attention to him, or I'll tear you apart. I don't know what your problem is with the man who has just arrived, but back off now!'

Although Saul is still almost foaming at the mouth with rage, he is scared of this giant of a man, who brings back memories of Goliath.[3] He calms down a little, and deliberately turns his back and walks away from David.

'Thank you, Samson,' says the Lord God. 'I don't need to tell you what a shock this must be to all of you, but now, I will explain everything. I am the Lord your God, and I have decided to bring you all here to spend the next seven days together. I have provided this luxury tent, food, drink and a place to bathe, but more of that later. Let me first introduce you to each other. Now, I have been close to each one of you throughout your lives. You certainly know me. From this moment on, you will call me the Lord God. I will be watching over you, as I always did.

'I have chosen the eleven of you to live together for the next seven days, because I want to see how you get on. I will set you tasks, in which you will either succeed or fail. You are all people that I have chosen to do my work over the centuries, and you arrived here in a particular order. Let me begin the introductions. The first person who walked through the gate today was the first woman on earth. This is Eve.'

Some sort of light shines down from the sky and hovers over Eve like a spotlight. The others stare at her in amazement.

'Do you all know me, or know of me?' asks Eve.

'Each one of us is descended from you, Eve,' says Moses.

'Yes, and it's thanks to you that my life has been so miserable,' shouts Saul. 'The sins I have committed are a result of your blasted actions in the garden of Eden. You brought sin and misery into the world. You ask us whether we have heard of you? Too right we have!'

Samson turns to Saul, about to give him another warning. Saul shuts up immediately. From her scared expression, Eve is obviously dumbstruck after Saul's outburst. Ruth walks over and pats her comfortingly on the shoulder.

'I have heard of you too, Eve,' says David. 'I don't know what the others think, but for a long time I held you responsible for bringing sin and suffering into the world. But I've come to realize that had I been the first person to live on this earth, I too would have fallen short of the glory of God. I've committed some terrible sins. It's a delight to meet you, the genuine "first lady".' He smiles at her warmly.

'Thank you for your kind words,' Eve replies shyly.

'I expect you all have a lot to say to Eve, but let's get on with the introductions,' says the voice of the Lord God. 'The second person who walked through the gate was Noah.' The light shines on him.

'The boat builder!' Joshua exclaims. 'I presume that because we are being introduced in order of our lives, everyone here has heard of you, except Eve.'

'You must have had such an adventure, Noah,' says Deborah. 'I grew up listening to many of the great stories of our ancestors, and the Flood was always my favourite. I hope you will share your experience with us.'

'I look forward to hearing your story as well,' bellows Samson. 'I also want to know why you saved some of the creatures that you did. Some of the insects that regularly bite and sting me, I don't find amusing. I'll discuss this with you later.'

'I know of Eve, but not the rest of you,' Noah replies. 'It's an honour that you have heard of me. I look forward to finding out about all of you, as I am sure you have equally good stories to tell.'

'The third person I wish to introduce—and I know that some will have heard of him already—is Joseph,' continues the Lord God. The dazzling light zooms round and picks out Joseph.

'So you're Joseph!' Moses exclaims. 'You brought the Hebrew people into Egypt to save them and, 400 years later, I had to lead them out of Egypt to save them. Doesn't the Lord work in mysterious ways? I look forward to chatting to you further.'

'As do I,' Joseph replies. 'I—'

'Maybe, if I have any nightmares, you can tell me what they mean,' interrupts Saul arrogantly. 'I too have heard of you, and I remember that you interpreted people's dreams. It should be interesting sharing our dreams with you.'

Samson glares at Saul. Once again Saul shuts up.

'It was the Lord God who helped me interpret dreams,' Joseph says quietly. 'If he wishes me to interpret dreams still, I will do so.'

The Lord God continues with the introductions. 'The next guest is Moses.' Again, the light moves, this time to highlight Moses.

Those who arrived after Moses gaze at him admiringly. Rahab steps up to him and says respectfully, 'It is a great honour to meet you. My name is Rahab. I lived in Jericho when Joshua and his army attacked the city to lead the Hebrews into the promised land. I've heard so much about you and all those wonderful miracles that you performed.'

'I've also heard of you,' says Samson. 'You're the chap who popped up a mountain and came down with the Lord God's Ten Commandments. I'm afraid I've broken every one of them. I do respect you, though, and when I was growing up I heard so many great stories about you. Let's hope you don't start making up a load of rules for us to live by here!' Samson seems to find this amusing, but Joseph, Eve and Noah look mystified.

Moses thanks Rahab for her warm welcome. Then he turns to Samson. 'I don't know who you are yet, but no one should boast about breaking any of the commandments, let alone all ten. As far as making rules is concerned, I don't make the rules. The Lord God is the one who does that.'

'I was only having a joke—just a friendly little poke,' Samson says, looking a little annoyed. During his lifetime he was well known for his fondness for practical jokes and riddles.[4]

'Enough!' shouts the voice of the Lord God. 'As you will realize by

14

now, the next guest is personally known to two of you here today. It's Joshua.' The light is now shining on him.

'And the walls came tumbling down,' sings Samson. The group have only been together for a short while, but already Samson is becoming a bit of a nuisance. No one really dares to say anything, though, because of his enormous size.

'Yes,' Joshua says shortly. 'They did come tumbling down.' He then pointedly turns away from Samson and looks at the rest of the group. 'I know these are just introductions,' he says, 'but it's a miracle that we are here today. To stand here with Eve and Noah— it's amazing! As you're all probably thinking yourselves, I have so much that I want to say and ask each one of you.'

'It's an honour to meet you, Joshua,' says Ruth.

'It's good to be here—I think,' Joshua replies. Some of the others giggle at this, obviously feeling the same way.

The mysterious light from the heavens shines on Rahab. 'This is Rahab,' booms the voice of the Lord God.

'I thought it might be you,' says Samson, 'the way you and Joshua hugged earlier. You were that prostitute who helped his spies.[5] If I need a little help later on, will you pop round?'

'Why are you here, big fellow?' asks David. 'I can see that everyone else here so far has been a true servant of God. You seem to be nothing but a troublemaker. Yes, Rahab was a prostitute, but she risked her life to help the Hebrews. She is a woman of great faith. That is what I have been taught about her.'

'I too have heard great things about Rahab,' adds Deborah. 'You spoke unkindly to her,' she says to Samson.

'You will do well to hold your tongue, Samson,' the Lord God's voice echoes around them.

'So you're Samson!' David exclaims, astonished. 'You're that brawling troublemaker who waged a one-man war against the Philistines. You must have killed thousands of them! I can't say you lived a very godly life, but I did enjoy hearing the stories about you destroying our old enemy.'[6]

'It seems that we all have a great deal to learn about each other,' says Noah. 'I'm beginning to understand why the Lord God has brought us together here.'

'I don't know about any of that,' Samson grunts. 'But, sorry, what's your name?' he asks David.

David tells him and Samson raises his eyebrows. 'If you fought those accursed Philistines as well, I look forward to hearing your stories. Perhaps we can share a few riddles about those heathen!'

'Attention, please!' comes the voice of the Lord God. 'We seem to have skipped someone. You now all know Samson.' The light moves to Deborah. 'But this is Deborah.'

'Another great leader!' Ruth says excitedly. 'I was taught that this woman was a national hero in Israel.[7] She roused the nation to action against the evil King Jabin from the north.'

'A great battle!' Saul nods, visibly impressed. 'I also remember hearing about your wonderful victory against Jabin's army.'

'I am delighted to be among such revered company,' Deborah responds, smiling.

The heavenly light then shines upon Ruth. 'This,' says the Lord God, 'is Ruth.'

'My great-grandmother!' David grins from ear to ear. 'I know all about that amazing love story between you and Boaz. I was told of your wonderful sense of responsibility to family and friends. These stories have always been such an encouragement and challenge for me. It's a miracle to be able to meet you.'

'The whole experience of being here is a mystery and miracle to me,' Ruth replies solemnly. 'If you are who you say you are, and you certainly seem to know about me, then I am truly delighted to meet my great-grandson.' They give each other a hug.

Saul, who is standing to one side looking quite miserable, is suddenly engulfed in the white light. 'This is Saul, the first king of Israel,' the Lord God announces.

'A king!' laughs Samson. 'I never obeyed many of your laws, Lord God, but one thing I have always known in my heart is that you were the only king for the Hebrew people. How did this *man* ever become a king?' Samson stares at Saul, who scowls at him.

'The people wanted a king,' he replies shortly. 'They wanted to be like other nations, and so I was anointed king by that great prophet Samuel.'[8]

'You can tell the others what sort of king you became, as well,' says the Lord God. 'Which leads me on to the final guest here today, the man who followed Saul as king of Israel, King David.'

'I am pleased to meet all you great people who lived before me,' David says, 'and who helped to shape our great nation.'

'Does that include me?' Saul interrupts.

'Perhaps we will be able to use this time to talk, Saul,' replies David.

'What is it with you two, anyway?' asks Joseph. 'Why are you so angry, Saul?'

'That's none of your business!' Saul snaps.

'Perhaps in time we'll come to understand the problem,' Deborah says soothingly.

'That concludes the introductions,' the Lord God announces. 'This is what will now happen. You will walk towards the large tent over there. Inside you will find a section prepared for the women to live in, and a section for the men. Another section in the tent will be where you can socialize, talk, eat and carry out the tasks that I set you. Outside the large tent are two very small tents, one for the women and one for the men. These will be for you to use for washing, for toilet functions and so on. There is a large pool outside the main tent, which you can all use to bathe in, and to cool down in these hot, desert conditions.'

The Lord God goes on to explain about food and eating. Fairly close to the communal pool is an area set aside for cooking, with a place for lighting the fire and an earthenware dish that can be inverted over the fire so that bread can be baked inside. God will provide them with much of the basic food that they are used to, such as olives, cheese, fruit and vegetables (mainly beans and lentils).

In a small pen nearby, they will find some goats, sheep and cattle, which will be a good source of milk and meat.[9] Close to the well, which will provide their drinking water, is growing a variety of trees, so that they can enjoy figs, pomegranates and other types of fruit. Near the huge wall, they will find a large nest of wild bees. Here they can (if they are careful!) collect honey. The Lord God has also provided a sack of salt. There are also plenty of skins of wine.

'Now that I have explained these things to you,' says the Lord God, 'I would like to welcome you here. In a couple of days, I will start asking you to vote for one person to leave the tent. If you are the one voted out, you will have to leave immediately, through the gate.

'As I have already mentioned, I will regularly set you small tasks to perform. You will all take part. If I am happy with the outcome of the task, you will be rewarded with extra food and wine. If you fail to complete the task successfully, you will have much of your food taken from you for a set period of time. So, learn to work together!

'Throughout your time here, you may speak to me whenever you wish, by entering a place set aside in the large tent. You can call this place the "Holy of Holies".'

Moses' jaw drops. He is shocked. 'Are you saying that any one of us can enter that most holy of places?' he asks the Lord God. You can tell by the expressions of some of the others that they fully understand why Moses has asked that question.[10]

'You are all equal here, and may speak with me whenever you wish,' comes the answer. 'I am the Lord your God and you are my children. Enter the Holy of Holies whenever you wish to speak to your Father in heaven.'

Moses and the others are speechless. Most of them have been used to the priests being the only people who can stand in the Lord's presence. What's happening here is all so much for them to take in at the moment.

The Lord God continues. 'Today, Day One, has certainly been quite a shock for you. I have no more to say to you now. Your first task will be set tomorrow morning. For the rest of today, you may settle into your new home. There are no limits to what you may eat or drink today. That will be all for now.'

'I like the sound of that honey by the wall,' Samson bursts out. 'Anyone fancy coming to get a bit? Reminds me of the time I killed that lion with my bare hands. Went back a few days later and found a swarm of bees inside the carcass. I scraped out loads of delicious honey.[11] Tasted great!'

'I've heard that story,' says David. 'I never thought it was true, not until now, looking at the size of you.'

Samson laughs and hurries over to the wall to find his honey. The others then start making their way slowly into the large tent to find out where they will be living and sleeping.

The two sleeping areas are clearly completely separate. The Lord God has left two huge signs above each area, saying, 'No men beyond this point' and 'No women beyond this point'. When David sees these signs, they remind him of the Bathsheba incident.[12] He knows he had better keep to the correct area!

In the women's area are four separate beds consisting of layers of tanned hides laid out on the floor. Each part of the tent is well lit by small lamps, each with two small holes, one for the wick and one to hold olive oil. When the oil is running low, the wick starts to smoulder, indicating that the lamp needs re-filling.[13]

The men's sleeping area is a little larger, with seven beds laid out.

As the others are surveying their new surroundings, Samson runs into the tent with a massive handful of honey. In the main communal area there are many earthenware pots set out, and he empties the honey into the nearest one he can find. He starts singing, 'Out of the wall came something to eat; thanks to those bees we have something sweet.'

The others hear the noise and come over to join him. The Lord God has provided the first loaf of bread. Samson asks them to break bread with him—to share a snack—and enjoy some of the delicious honey. This seems like a good idea, so they all wash their hands by pouring water over them from a large jug, which Ruth has thoughtfully filled from the well outside.[14]

Samson is just about to take the bread and break it when Moses stops him. 'Haven't we forgotten something, Samson?'

'We have bread. We have honey,' Samson replies. 'What more do we want?'

'A prayer of thanksgiving, perhaps?' Moses answers.

The others immediately agree. With their heads bowed, Moses says, 'Blessed are you, our God, King of the world, who provides us with bread from the earth.' Then they all take pieces of the bread and dip it into the honey. It's just what they need after an amazing and confusing few hours.

After the meal, Moses offers another prayer of thanks to the Lord God. Things are pretty quiet after this, and understandably so. Everyone seems to be taking in the situation and reflecting on it. Certainly, in time, they will have a great deal to talk about, but for now they need to settle in.

Eventually Joshua breaks the silence by announcing that it is getting near the end of the day, and it is time to bathe.[15]

At that moment as well, almost instinctively, Rahab says that she will begin to prepare the evening meal.[16] The other women immediately offer their help, as they are all used to the idea that it is traditionally the women's role to prepare food.

'Shall I slaughter a sheep for you, Rahab?' Noah asks. Rahab thanks him for this offer, and he disappears to do the job. The meat will be boiled as part of a stew, with beans, lentils and other vegetables added.

While the women are cooking, the others either bathe or stroll around the tent, collecting their thoughts. Saul spends much of the time staring at David, but from a distance. He is clearly wondering how he is going to survive the next few days in the same tent and sleeping quarters as his old enemy.

Samson is happily splashing around in the communal pool outside, drinking wine and singing to himself.

During the next few hours, not a great deal happens. The women finish cooking the stew and they all sit down at the table to eat. It's a fairly long, low table, with eleven cushions positioned along the sides. They sit in silence for a moment at the beginning of the meal, waiting for someone to offer a prayer of thanksgiving.

Eventually it is Moses who repeats the blessing that he said earlier.

Perhaps because it is the first day, they are all a little shocked and tired, so not much is said during the meal. Samson, however, drinks a great deal of wine and leaves the table early, taking an extra skinful of wine with him. He staggers outside and sits down under one of the fruit trees. His voice floats back into the tent, singing a song about Philistines and how he has slaughtered so many.

The women are particularly quiet throughout the meal. When everyone has eaten, they go about clearing up. Not long afterwards, they start making their way to their sleeping area. From his resting place under the tree, Samson sees them on their way to bed and shouts out, 'Hey, Eve! Come and drink some wine with me, then maybe I can tempt you into something! You like a bit of temptation, don't you?'

Eve looks appalled at this clumsy suggestion. Shaking their heads in disgust, the other women gather round to console her, and together they disappear into their sleeping area.

'What is it with you? David shouts to Samson. 'How did God ever choose someone like you to do his work? You sit there all evening getting drunk; you've upset Eve.'

Samson just takes another swig of wine and laughs.

Eventually, most of the men go off to their beds, while Samson falls asleep outside, quite drunk. Only Saul doesn't go to bed straight away. He seems quite depressed and troubled, and stays at the table for a while, drinking a good bit of wine himself.

Noah pops out after another hour has passed and asks Saul what the problem is, and why there is such tension between him and David. Saul is in no mood to speak. 'Get away from me!' he shouts at Noah who, realizing that there is no point in trying to talk to him at the moment, goes back to bed.

As Saul sits there, wallowing in his own misery, he suddenly starts laughing to himself. He gets up, walks into the cooking area and finds a sharp knife. He then slips into the men's sleeping area and heads towards David, who is fast asleep. Gently taking hold of the bottom of David's robe, Saul cuts off a large piece of cloth with the knife.

'Two can play at that game,' Saul murmurs to himself.[17] This seems to cheer him up. He returns the knife to the cooking area, drinks a little more wine and wanders outside the tent. Passing Samson, he finds another tree and lies down beneath it. Soon, he too is fast asleep.

DAY TWO

At about nine in the morning, the Lord God's voice echoes round the tent. 'Rise up from your sleep! That includes you, Samson! You all have time to wash and freshen yourselves up before coming to the table. After you've eaten your breakfast, I will give you today's instructions.'

Some of the women are already up and have prepared some food to eat. There is freshly baked bread on the table, some of the honey that Samson found the day before, figs, grapes, pomegranates and some milk.

As David walks towards the men's washing area, he notices that a huge chunk has been cut from the hem of his robe. 'Saul! What in— what is wrong with you?' he yells. The other men stare at David, shocked. What on earth is he talking about? Why is there a big piece of cloth missing from his robe? Why is he screaming about Saul?

David sprints off round the back of the tent, looking for Saul. The others follow right behind, extremely curious. They noticed the strange tension between the two men yesterday, and are dying to discover what this is all about.

David finds Saul outside, lying still half-asleep under his tree. 'What is wrong with you, Saul?' he asks angrily. 'Why do you hate me so much? I always treated you as my king, the Lord God's chosen king, and just wanted to serve you. Back in the Wild Goat Rocks[18] I could have easily killed you, and at Mount Hachilah.[19] But I always showed you nothing but respect, and yet you spent your whole life tracking me down to kill me. As a young lad, I played the harp for you when you were depressed and in a dark mood. You told me I was the only one who could help you when you were feeling down. So why all this hatred from you? What have I done?'

Saul says nothing. If anything, David's tirade seems to make him feel even worse.

'David's question sounds like a very fair one,' Deborah remarks. Some of the women have joined the men standing round Saul.

'I think so too,' adds Joseph. 'Saul, I heard you talking in your sleep last night. You seem so troubled. Did you have any disturbing dreams? If so, I may be able to interpret them with the Lord God's help and, by doing that, we might find out what is upsetting you so deeply.'

'None of you can help me,' Saul says gloomily. 'Anyway, can anyone tell me why I am here? The last thing I remember is falling on my sword on Mount Gilboa.[20] I didn't ask to be here!'

'None of us did,' says Ruth. 'But we are here, and we are all people whom the Lord God chose to do his work. We should try to talk, and maybe resolve our difficulties.'

'Just give them both a sword and let them fight to the death and be done with it,' shouts Samson. He has finally woken and come over to join the others, although he is looking a little rough.

'That won't solve anything,' Eve retorts. 'Let's just gather round the table and eat.'

'OK,' says Samson, 'as long as you tell us where you got the fruit from. You haven't been to any forbidden trees this morning, have you?'

'I would say "Grow up", Samson,' Joseph exclaims, 'but I don't think you could get any bigger if you tried. Why can't you leave Eve alone, or at least talk to her and find out what it was actually like at the beginning of the world?'

Before anyone can say anything else, they hear the Lord God announcing, 'Eat your meal now, in silence. Ruth will say the blessing. After you have eaten, I want you to gather in the communal bathing pool. It will be particularly hot today, and this will be the coolest place for you to meet. When you are in the pool, I will explain the first task.'

Although it's only mid-morning, the sun is blazing down already. The pool is definitely the best place to be!

After the prayer of thanksgiving, they eat. Samson looks as if he is eating enough for ten people, devouring a vast amount of bread and honey. He also manages to eat five pomegranates.

Following their silent breakfast, they leave the table, dressed suitably—the men covering themselves from the waist down, and the women wearing robes of closely woven cloth, and step into the large pool outside. There are quite a few trees around the pool, providing a bit of shade, and the water is enjoyably cool and refreshing. The women sit together at one end, but the men arrange themselves separately, although Joshua and Moses are side by side. As you might guess, Saul and David are pretty much on opposite ends of the pool, although it was Saul who made a conscious effort to position himself as far away from David as he could.

'This is the Lord your God.' His voice suddenly echoes around them. 'This is your first task. While you are sitting here in the pool, you are all to ask *one* question from anyone you choose. You may ask any question you wish, and you can choose anyone to ask. You must answer whatever questions you are asked, and do so honestly. Remember that I am the Lord your God and I know everything.

'Yesterday, Eve was the first to arrive and David the last so, for this task, David will be the first to choose someone and ask his question. Eve will be the last. You may have a few moments to think; then begin in your own time.'

The general reaction to this announcement is one of discomfort. They all appear to be asking themselves, 'What on earth am I going to ask? Who shall I ask?'

After a while, David declares himself ready. 'This probably won't surprise any of you,' he begins, 'but my question is for Saul.'

'This should be fun!' Samson guffaws.

'Let's stick to the rules, Samson,' says Moses. 'Don't interrupt.'

'You and your rules—your "commandments"!' Samson retorts. 'Is that all you ever think about?'

'My question to Saul,' David continues loudly, 'is this. What on earth was your problem with me? Why the insane jealousy and attempts to kill me, and the deceit and lies?'

'I've got nothing to say,' Saul mutters.

Rahab gives Saul a hard stare. 'Just tell him the truth. We've all seen that there is some terrible problem between you and David. Just tell us about it. Like the Lord God said, tell the truth.'

'Go on, Saul,' adds Eve.

'You can be quiet, for a start!' Saul snaps at Eve. 'You're the one who messed it up for us in the beginning. If anyone's to blame for my problems, it's you!'

'That's completely uncalled for!' says Deborah, frowning. 'You must answer the question.'

Silence falls. Everyone's eyes are on Saul.

'"Saul has killed thousands, but David has killed tens of thousands",'[21] Saul suddenly blurts out. 'That's what the women started singing after David killed the giant Goliath. I was jealous. I was the king. The way those women were singing, David might as well have been king. That's the simple answer to your question, David. Before you killed Goliath, you used to come and play the harp and sing to me when I felt down. I used to love your visits and I became very fond of you. You know how low I used to feel; well, when those women started to sing your praises, it made me feel down again and I admit that I became insanely jealous of you. I didn't trust you, and started to think that you were after my throne. As time went by, I noticed how the people had started to love and admire you. You were a great leader—I knew that in my heart—but my jealousy hid it from my eyes. I hate to say it, but I wanted you dead.'

'I only ever saw you as my king,' David replies gently. 'I only ever wanted to serve you. I knew all about your plots to try and kill me. Jonathan told me everything.'

'Who is Jonathan?' asks Rahab.

'He was Saul's son,' David continues. 'Saul, you were happy for me to marry your daughter Michal. I was to fight in your army as part of the condition. You hoped I would die in battle.[22] You then went mad and spent all your time, if not the rest of your life, trying to hunt me down and kill me, and yet I simply wanted to serve you.

As you well know, I even had the chance to kill you a couple of times, but I spared your life.'[23]

Saul just shakes his head, gazing at David. 'That's what angered me even more. You were always so nicely spoken and popular. I hated it. As I've told you, I became more and more jealous. You asked me a question and now I've answered it. I don't wish to discuss it any further.'

'I appreciate you answering,' David replies, 'but I still fail to understand why I upset you so much. Perhaps we can talk more later.'

Joseph then turns to Saul and says, 'I believe it's your turn to ask a question now, Saul. Who are you going to ask?'

'Why do I have to talk again?' Saul responds petulantly. 'I'm fed up with this game.'

'Looks like you'd better sing him a song, David, and calm him down,' jokes Samson. Ruth stands up, wades over to Saul, and puts a tentative hand on his shoulder. 'It's difficult for all of us here, Saul. Please follow the Lord God's instructions and ask your question.' This gesture seems to do the trick. Saul calms down a bit.

'Can you come over here and calm me down as well?' Samson shouts over to Ruth.

'Have you no respect for anything?' Moses bursts out angrily. 'I don't know why you are here. Just follow the rules, please.'

Samson simply laughs.

Silence falls again. It's time for Saul's question.

Saul fixes his gaze on Samson. 'Hey, you, the big man! Like Moses said, why are you here? I heard the stories about you and your incredible strength. Why didn't you destroy the Philistines once and for all, and why didn't you behave more like a man of God? You were a Nazarite, after all!'[24]

'Now listen, your Majesty!' Samson is annoyed. 'Don't you talk to me about behaving like a man of God! From what I've heard so far, you didn't do much better, with your crazy jealousy and your murder plans! OK, so I forgot my vows. I drank, slept around, and yes, I pretty much broke every commandment that our dear Moses set all those years before; sorry, mate.' Samson glances towards Moses. He continues, 'I killed thousands of Philistines single-handedly. Most of my fellow Hebrews were too scared to fight. Many of them carried on worshipping false gods. I did many things wrong, but always acknowledged that there was only one God, who blessed me with superhuman strength. Anyway, I'm not a good speaker, so that's it!'

Ruth waves her hand, indicating that she wishes to speak. 'I lived just after Samson was alive and, despite thinking that he had been a fool, and despite his behaviour with us here so far, I would like to say a few words now and speak up for him, to help answer Saul's question.'

'Why, thank you, Ruth darling,' says Samson with a cheeky grin.

Blushing, Ruth goes on, 'We know that Samson was blessed with amazing physical strength, but when I lived with my people, many talked about the other gifts he possessed. Though you wouldn't think it, having met him only yesterday, Samson also has a remarkable psychological and spiritual strength. Did you know that he spent 20 lonely years as a resistance leader?[25] Samson did have an eye for the women, but one of his relationships, with a woman called Delilah, ended in catastrophe.'

'I know that story,' interrupts David. 'She betrayed him to the Philistine leaders. Despite all your strength, Samson, it was your weakness with the women that led to your downfall.'

Ruth continues. 'In spite of the catastrophe of his betrayal, having his eyes put out, and the degradation he endured at the hands of the Philistines, he did not break. Many of us would have done. This man didn't,' she says, pointing at Samson. 'While in prison, he came to recognize the error of his ways and asked the Lord God for forgiveness. Each one of us here today knows that it's a repentant heart that the Lord God wants—it's then that we receive forgiveness. Samson was forgiven and the Lord God gave him his strength back one last time. With this final gift, Samson destroyed the temple of Dagon. In doing so, he killed more Philistines than he had ever done before. Samson also sacrificed his own life by doing this.

'We are all made in the image of the Lord God. I believe that Samson faithfully reflects something of his maker. He represents in human form something of the power and strength of the Lord God himself.'

No one says a word. Even Samson just sits there, pondering on what he's heard. Everybody is amazed at what Ruth has had to say.

Ruth speaks again. 'I believe it's me who asks the next question. I know that many here are longing to speak to Eve. Some of us have made some nasty comments already, blaming her for all the problems and evil in life. I think it's only fair that Eve should tell us her own story. My question to you, Eve, is about what it was like in the very beginning. Of course we know the story, but can you tell us what it was really like and what went wrong?'

All eyes turn to Eve, who looks very uncomfortable. Suddenly she starts to cry quietly. The other women move closer to comfort her. After a while, she manages to compose herself and opens her mouth to reply.

'I'm sorry to interrupt,' Joshua says abruptly, 'but I think Eve should know what reports we have heard about her, and why we think it was she who brought sin into the world. We may be wrong, Eve, but this is what we have been led to believe. I'm sure the others here, like me, were taught that you represented everything about a woman that a good man should guard against. I was taught that women are by nature disobedient, guileless, weak-willed, always prone to temptation and evil, deceitful—'

'Tell me about it!' breaks in Samson.

'Anyway,' Joshua continues, ignoring the interruption, 'that's what we've been brought up to believe. It's only fair that you know that, Eve. Now you can tell us your story.'

Swallowing hard, she makes a start. 'Yesterday, we were amazed at how we came to be here in this place. We don't know how it happened. It was like that with Adam and myself. It was the Lord God who created us. We discovered that we came into existence on the sixth day, at the very beginning of time, objects of a unique act of creation.

'Adam and I were there in the garden as equals. It was glorious. Try to think of a time in your lives when you felt totally happy and at peace with all around you, with the whole universe as well, and at one with God. That's what it was like in the beginning. It wasn't a feeling that came only fleetingly, though—it was constant, wonderful. The Lord God created the heavens and the earth purely as an act of love. He made it clear to Adam and to me that we were to be part of this creation. We were asked to look after his world and bring it under our control.

'The Lord God took us to the garden of Eden. He asked us to look after it and cultivate it. We could eat any of the fruit in the garden, but we weren't to touch any fruit from one tree, the tree that gave knowledge of what was good and what was bad. God told us that we would die if we ate that fruit.'

'Is it true that you and Adam ran around naked?' interrupts Samson, sniggering. One or two of the others also smirk at this.

'That's how the Lord God created us in the very beginning,' Eve replies simply. 'We didn't know we were naked. It was the original way God wanted us to be. We weren't ashamed or embarrassed. It was beautiful and natural.'

'So when did you become ashamed?' asks Noah slowly. 'This is getting to the heart of things, I think—the big question of what went wrong.'

'I must make clear to you,' Eve goes on, 'that I may have been the very first person on this earth, but I am no different from any of you here. Things were perfect in the beginning, but I still had a mind of my own, my own free will, as we all do.

'One afternoon, after a wonderful morning with Adam, I went for a walk in the beautiful garden. Like any of us here, I liked some time on my own. I wandered up to the tree of the knowledge of good and evil, and gazed at it for a while. I began to think about what the Lord God might have meant when he said it would give us knowledge of everything. As I stood there pondering this, I saw a huge snake slithering slowly past the tree. Then it stopped and looked right at me. I don't know why, but I began to feel that the snake was talking to me, saying, "Go on, try some of the fruit." I kept telling myself that I shouldn't, that I would die. Again I imagined the snake speaking to me. "Go on, eat some of the fruit. You won't die. In fact, you'll become like God and know what's right or wrong."

'I looked at the fruit and it certainly seemed more beautiful than all the other fruit in the garden. I eventually convinced myself that it wouldn't cause any harm if I tried just a bit of it. I said to myself, "What harm could come if I know the difference between good and evil?" I tasted some. It was delicious.

'My next thought was to share it with Adam. I didn't want to tempt him or deceive him. I loved him and simply wanted to share the fruit with him. As soon as he had eaten it, though, everything changed. It was an awful feeling. I felt physically sick with guilt. Adam and I stared at each other, and we realized that we were naked. We were so ashamed and embarrassed. We found some huge fig leaves, quickly sewed a few together with tough stalks of grass, and covered ourselves. I felt terrible. If this was what it was like to have knowledge of good and evil, I wanted none of it.

'Remember, though—I made a mistake. All of you here, by the sound of it, have made mistakes. I say again, I am no different from any of you. I may have been the first human being, but I am only human. God gave us the freedom to choose what is right and wrong. It would seem that each one of us falls short of the glory of God.'[26]

No one speaks. How can anyone dispute this? Everyone looks lost in their own thoughts, reflecting on their lives and how they have let the Lord God down in so many different ways.

'This is the Lord God!' The voice suddenly fills the air. 'So far, so good. We will continue with this task at the same time tomorrow morning, when Samson will ask the next question. The next few hours are your own. Later in the day, it will be the duty of the men to prepare the meal and serve the women.'

There is a general groan from some of the men, but their resigned faces show that they accept the fact that the Lord God must be obeyed.

The women leave the pool together. Rahab, Deborah and Ruth continue questioning Eve about Adam and the beginning. They are fascinated and want to hear more. Samson wades over to David in the pool and they start to swap Philistine stories. Samson is really impressed with David's story about Goliath. Saul is close enough to hear what they are talking about. When he hears the name 'Goliath', his jealousy begins to take over again, so he stomps out of the pool, goes inside the tent and lies down.

Moses and Joshua relive some of their adventures in the wilderness. Noah has gone off and found some fallen branches lying under one of the trees; he has started to build something, but there's no clue what it is. Joseph sits near him, watching quietly.

A few hours later, Samson announces that he is hungry. He tells the others that he is going to gather some more honey from the bees he had found in the outer wall. Moses suggests that it would be a good time to prepare the meal as the Lord God has instructed.

'Let's take a calf from the herd over there,' Noah suggests. 'We'll cook the meat, have some milk, make some cream, use some of the honey that Samson brings back. It should be a fine meal.'

'Don't forget the wine!' shouts Samson, returning with huge pawfuls of honey. His face is already covered in the sticky stuff.

'We won't forget the wine,' David laughs. 'Although it might do you good, Samson, to forget it for a change!'

Even Saul decides to help out this time. It is he who slaughters the calf and cuts up the meat. Is he doing it to help out, or is he imagining that the calf he is butchering is David? The other men just let him get on with it.

The women have decided to have another dip in the communal pool to cool off. 'The men appear to be coping without our help,' Rahab says with a grin. The other women smile with her. Even Eve seems more comfortable now. She asks, 'Do you think the men may have changed their perception of me a little?'

'Of course they must have,' replies Ruth. 'Listening to you speak this morning got us thinking. Any one of us would have taken that fruit in the garden of Eden. We all know that in our hearts. You would be a fool if you declared that you would have simply obeyed God and never touched the forbidden fruit. We are servants of God —even Samson!—and we are human, which means that we fail God every day, whether it's you, me or any one of us. To answer your question, Eve, of course the men have changed their perception of you.'

'I might ask them myself during the meal,' Eve says, half to herself.

'Good for you, my girl,' says Deborah approvingly. They laugh together.

It's time for the meal, and they all gather around the table. Saul asks Eve to say the blessing, and it's obvious that she is pleased with this request. They begin to tuck into a fine meal, and David serves wine.

The conversation flows naturally, many of them finding out more about each other in a relaxed way. Samson suddenly bursts out with something that first confuses everyone and then has them in fits of laughter. As they are chatting away, he turns to Eve. 'Eve, excuse my bluntness, but if you were the first woman on earth, do you have a belly button?'

Everyone's first reaction is to look at Samson as the fool again, but then they realize that, as daft as it sounds, it's an interesting question. There is laughter round the table.

'I don't know much about the human body,' continues Samson, 'but I know about babies being born, and I know they are attached to their mothers by some sort of cord that goes into the stomach. As you were the first woman on earth, I just wondered whether you had a belly button.'

Eve does not reply. She blushes deeply at having been asked such an intimate question. Some of the other men start discussing the matter, though, wondering in general terms whether the first man and women would need belly buttons. After a few minutes, Deborah interjects to say that Samson's question is in very poor taste and they should change the subject at once. They finish eating in silence.

At the end of the meal, Joseph turns to David. 'We heard earlier that you can sing and play the harp,' he says. 'There's no harp here, but could you sing us a song of thanksgiving after this delicious meal?'

'Do you really want me to ruin a fine evening?' replies David with a chuckle.

'Don't be so modest,' says Deborah briskly, looking over at David. 'I think you should sing us a song.'

'Very well.' David gives in to the pressure. 'This is one of many songs I wrote when I was king of Israel.' He begins to sing:

> *O God, have mercy on us and bless us.*
> *Please look on us with kindness,*
> *so that the whole world may know your will,*
> *And so that all the nations may know your salvation.*
> *May all the peoples praise you O God;*
> *And again I say may all the peoples praise you!*
>
> *May all the nations be glad and sing for joy,*
> *For you are a just God, and guide every nation on earth.*
>
> *May all the peoples praise you, O God;*
> *And again I say, may all the peoples praise you!*
>
> *The land has produced its wonderful harvest;*
> *God, our God has truly blessed us.*
> *God has blessed us.*
> *May people everywhere honour him.*[27]

More than a few eyes are filled with tears after the song. 'Amen! Amen!' says Moses loudly.

'That was beautiful,' Eve murmurs. Some of them notice that even Saul has tears in his eyes after the song, and for the first time he seems relaxed and even a little more at ease around David. The music really does seem to soothe Saul's dark moods. It is quite ironic, really, that as much as he appears to want David dead, at the same time he desperately needs David to soothe his soul with this heavenly music.

After a moment, Moses stands up and says to the others, 'That was an excellent meal, and a fine song to finish, David. Can I now suggest that we establish a few rules about who is to clear up and prepare the food each day?'

'Come on, Moses,' laughs David. 'Where do you think you are, Mount Sinai? You may have helped to make the rules back then, but please don't start here!'

A few of the others join in the laughter, but Joseph, Noah and Eve still don't get the joke. David explains to them about Moses and the receiving of the Ten Commandments, and tells them what they were. 'So, you see, Moses is known as the great law giver,' he concludes, 'which is why we find it amusing that he is even trying to make rules about who should cook and clean here.' Understanding smiles dawn on the faces of Joseph, Noah and Eve.

Day Two is coming to a close. After the meal, a few of the group make their way to the sleeping areas. Some stay up for a while to chat and drink a little more wine.

Interestingly, Samson is chatting away with Rahab and, for once, is behaving himself. He is keen to hear in full her story about the two spies and the destruction of Jericho. Their conversation continues for quite a while. Is Samson really behaving himself, or is he trying his luck with Rahab? After all, Samson is still Samson!

DAY THREE

After a good night's sleep and a fine breakfast of fruit, milk and honey, the characters gather in the communal pool for the continuation of the first task. It is already very hot, so yet again the pool is cooling and pleasant for them all.

The Lord God doesn't need to say anything. They know the routine. Everybody looks at Samson, waiting for him to begin his question. He is in fine form again, chirpy and chuckling to himself as he starts to speak. The others wonder what on earth he is about to say.

He begins, 'I'm still fascinated about Eve being the first person on earth, but before I ask my question, there's a few points I'd like to make. First, I can imagine that when Adam and Eve were expelled from the garden of Eden, they felt really "put out"!' Everyone laughs. Even Eve sees the funny side and smiles. She has realized that Samson is a joker and enjoys his riddles and puns. Samson continues, 'I can imagine Adam's children asking him why they don't live in the garden of Eden any more, and him answering, "Because your mother ate us out of house and home!"' Again the others laugh their heads off. Whatever they think of Samson, he certainly has a wit, even if it is a fairly blunt instrument. Before they have managed to compose themselves, he adds, 'You know, last night before I went to sleep, I was thinking how lucky Adam was—the man didn't have a mother-in-law!' This really cracks everyone up.

'Samson, get on with your question and follow the rules!' the Lord God booms.

'Was that the Lord God or Moses talking?' Samson says, to another gale of laughter.

Finally he gets on with his question. 'Sorry about all that, Eve, I can't help myself sometimes. In a way, my question has something to do with what I was asking yesterday about whether you have a belly button. I am still intrigued about how it all happened in the beginning. At what age were you created? Were you created as a baby, a young girl or what? Were you aware of your age when you were created? I'm sorry, that seems to be more than one question…'

'Don't worry,' Eve breaks in. 'I think I know what you're trying to ask me. I'll try to explain it as simply as I can. I certainly wasn't created as a baby. I suppose Adam and I were created as a young man and woman. As I said yesterday, we simply came into existence. We were immediately aware of our love for each other and our love for the Lord God, our creator. We both had a wonderful sense of innocence, which was ruined by the wrong choice I made.'

'Remember, Eve,' Joseph interjects, 'any one of us here would probably have chosen to do the same.'

'Thank you, Joseph,' Eve replies. 'I've begun to understand that it was this innocence that was the great issue. There were two wonderful trees in Eden. The first was the tree of life, which I now understand symbolized the immortality that Adam and I had been born into. The other tree was, of course, the tree of the knowledge of good and evil. The fact that these trees were there at all implies that there was some sort of test. The wonderful life of Eden obviously had a condition attached, namely that the fruit of the tree of good and evil should never be eaten.'

'So why do you think the Lord God put it there?' asks Moses.

Noah attempts to answer Moses' question. 'It would seem to me that the Lord God intended Adam and Eve to have a real choice about whether they ate the fruit or not. I believe that he wanted them to live in dependence on him, and only in this way could they remain truly innocent. I believe that he has always required a child-like obedience of us.'

Eve continues, 'There are obviously some kinds of knowledge that only the Lord God should have, and it's not for us to search for it. We should accept that this is in our own best interests.'

'If only you had made the right choice,' says Saul miserably.

'Why don't you choose to snap out of your misery?' Joseph retorts.

Samson thanks Eve for her answer.

Deborah then announces, 'I believe it's my turn to ask a question.' She turns and looks at Ruth. 'I would like you to share your story with us, if you don't mind. You have not said very much, Ruth, and I would like to know why the Lord God chose you to come to this place with the rest of us.'

'I'm afraid I don't have much to tell.' Ruth looks down modestly.

'That's nonsense!' David exclaims. 'You are my great-grandmother, and I was brought up hearing many wonderful things about you. If you don't mind, Deborah, I would like to say a few words about this remarkable woman!'

Deborah nods in agreement. Ruth seems a little uncomfortable, but David proceeds.

'A man named Elimelech, my great-great-grandfather, I believe, was married to a woman called Naomi. Elimelech took his family from their home in Bethlehem to go and live in Moab, a foreign country. You may be interested to know that the original Moab was the son of an incestuous relationship between a man called Lot and his oldest daughter (Lot was drunk at the time), and as a nation the Moabites were Israel's enemies, having opposed Israel when she came out of Egypt.'

'I remember them well!' Moses shakes his head.

David continues, 'After Elimelech died, his sons married two local girls. Chilion married Orpah, and Mahlon married Ruth. Ten years later, though, the two sons died as well, and their mother Naomi decided to go back to Bethlehem. She asked her two daughters-in-law to go back and live with their own mothers. They both refused. In the end, Orpah decided to go, but Ruth would not leave Naomi. The words she said to Naomi, so I was taught, were: "Don't ask me to leave you! Let me go with you. Wherever you go, I will go; wherever you live, I will live. Your people will be my people, and your God will be my God. Wherever you die, I will die, and that is where I will be buried."'[28]

'And you said you had no story to tell!' Eve exclaims with tears in her eyes.

'That's one heck of a great-grandmother you've got there, David!' adds Samson.

Deborah asks Ruth if she would like to continue her story herself. She replies, 'Again, I don't believe there's much to tell. When we got to Bethlehem, the barley harvest had just started. I asked Naomi if I could gather the grain that the harvest workers left, and she said I could. I ended up working in a field belonging to a rich and influential man called Boaz. He happened to belong to the family of Naomi's late husband, Elimelech. When I eventually met him, he was very kind to me, extremely kind. I asked him why he was treating me so well, and I was amazed to discover that he already knew a great deal about me. He told me I had a wonderful and pure heart. He told me how courageous he thought I'd been to make the sacrifice to follow Naomi and the Lord God.'

'Don't forget to tell us that he then invited you out for lunch!' laughs David.

'Oh, it wasn't like that, David,' Ruth replies, blushing.

'Of course it was! Yes, he was kind to you because of the wonderful things you had done, but he was also in love with you. That's how I heard it!'

'Now you're embarrassing me, David,' Ruth frowns. 'To sum it all up, Boaz and I were married, and I gave birth to a son called Obed.'

'Who gave birth to Jesse, and Jesse gave birth to me,' David finishes, proudly.

Saul groans quietly in the background. The others give him annoyed glances.

Rahab then speaks up. 'I believe it's now me to ask a question. I'd like to direct my question to David. The reason I've chosen you is because of a dream I had last night. I remember on Day One that somebody mentioned about Joseph having the ability to interpret dreams. I told my dream to Joseph just before breakfast this morning. I can't remember all the details now, but I do remember seeing you on the roof of a palace.[29] In the distance I saw a naked woman bathing, and then I suddenly saw a man dying in battle.

'When I told Joseph about my dream, he said that I must ask you about it today, David. He says that the dream refers to a terrible mistake you made in your life. Could you explain what it might mean?'

David's face goes white. Rahab's dream seems to have touched a raw nerve.

Moses nods slowly. 'This should be interesting. So far, King Saul has been getting all the bad press. What's your story, David?'

'Yes! What's your story, David?' asks Saul who has risen to his feet, fists clenched.

'Joseph was right when he said it refers to a terrible mistake I made in my life,' David answers slowly. 'In fact, Rahab, your dream was about something that was possibly the darkest event in my life.'

'Come on, David,' interrupts Samson. 'Tell us about it! I'm sure it's not that bad. We've all got our own stories of dark events. I messed up pretty bad, Eve ate the fruit, Saul's a loony! Just tell us your story.'

Saul gives Samson an evil stare, but the big man just grins back. David continues, 'I know we each have our own stories to tell, but when you have to speak about one of your own sins to others, it seems as if it's the worst sin that anyone could commit. It was a terrible thing that I did.

'The pictures in Rahab's dream are quite accurate. I was king. One spring afternoon, after I had had a nap, I went out on to the palace roof to stretch and stroll around. As I was walking about, I looked down and saw a beautiful woman taking a bath on a secluded part of her roof-top.'

'I like this story already!' interrupts Samson.

'Let him speak, Samson,' Deborah says to Samson angrily. She seems to scare him a little and—unusually—he shuts up.

David goes on, 'I found out that this woman was called Bathsheba. She was married to a man called Uriah, but even so I sent for her to be brought to the palace. I slept with her—and yes,

Moses, I can see the way you're looking at me; I know what one of the commandments states!'

Looking shocked, Ruth says, 'So you committed adultery, David?'

'That's just the beginning,' David replies wretchedly. 'It's gets a great deal worse.' All eyes are glued on him. 'I later found out that she was pregnant.'

'Oh dear,' says Joseph quietly.

'Oh dear, oh dear!' says Saul, who looks as if he is thoroughly enjoying the story. Listening to David retelling a sin apparently cheers him up even more than listening to David's music.

'I'm not proud of any of this,' David mutters. 'Remember, others of you may have to share some terrible sin that you have committed. This is not easy.'

'Please continue,' Eve says soothingly.

David takes a deep breath. 'Bathsheba's husband was away fighting with the army against the Ammonites, another of our enemies. I sent for him. My plan was to let him go home to his wife. He would then sleep with her and assume that the baby was his, and that would be the end of the story. Well, Uriah was a good man. He didn't go to his wife. He made it clear that he was fighting a holy war, and it wasn't right to go home to eat, drink and sleep with his wife when the other men of Israel were away fighting. The following day I tried to get him to go home again. This time I got him drunk, but he still wouldn't go.'

'This is terrible.' Joseph looks deeply shocked.

'I'm afraid it gets even worse, Joseph,' David replies. 'When I realized that Uriah wasn't going to visit his wife, I did a truly evil thing. I sent Uriah back to battle with a letter for Joab, the commanding officer. This letter instructed Joab to put Uriah in the front line where the fighting was worst. My plan was to have Uriah killed in battle—and that's exactly what happened.

'Bathsheba was obviously devastated at Uriah's death and she mourned for him. When her period of mourning was over, I sent for her to come to the palace, and she became my wife. She gave birth to a son. The Lord God was not at all pleased about any of this.'

'I'm not surprised!' Joshua shakes his head vigorously. 'An adulterer and a murderer! That's one of the worst things I've heard for a long time. You appal me, David.'

David continues in a low voice, 'Now you can make sense of your dream, Rahab. I was disgusted with what I had done. My prophet Nathan made it very clear to me that I had committed a terrible sin. I truly repented, and I did receive the Lord God's forgiveness but, as a punishment, the son that was born to me became very ill and died.'[30]

'It's certainly a shock to hear your story,' Moses says thoughtfully. 'But if the Lord God forgave you, then we should all forgive you, as we too have been forgiven.'

'I'm sure none of us has been as bad as that, though!' shouts Saul. 'I know you all think ill of me here, but now you can see that David is no angel!'

'David has repented!' Deborah retorts. 'Have you ever repented, Saul?' He falls silent, glaring at her.

At this point, as emotions are getting quite heated, the Lord God makes an announcement: 'The final part of this task will take place at the same time tomorrow morning, when Joshua will ask his question first. Over the next hour or so now, I will be inviting you individually to come into the Holy of Holies, where you can talk to me about anything. Eve, you will be first. Put on some dry clothes and then come to the Holy of Holies.'

As Eve leaves the pool, the others either talk quietly to their neighbours or leave to go and eat some fruit or drink some water from the well.

A short while later, Eve enters the Holy of Holies. It's a small area, with a comfortable seat in the middle. In here, the voice of the Lord God is softer, more friendly. 'How's it all going, Eve?'

After a few moments to reflect, Eve answers. 'We're still bewildered as to why we are here and how we got here. I've found it difficult to realize that everyone knows about me, and yet I know none of them. I feel ashamed and guilty that many of them think it's totally my fault that there is sin and evil in the world. I know they appear generous and supportive to me now, but I do wonder what some of them really think deep down. But you're the Lord God, and I'm not going to question you. You've brought me here for a reason, and I'll just follow your instructions.'

'So you are happy to continue, Eve?' the Lord God asks.

'Yes, Lord,' she answers. The Lord God tells her that she may now leave the Holy of Holies. As she walks out, Deborah catches sight of her and says, 'That was quick!'

'I didn't have that much to say,' Eve replies.

The Lord God then calls out, 'Will Noah please come to the Holy of Holies.'

Noah walks in and takes a seat. The Lord God asks him how he is finding the situation. Noah replies, 'I've seen many of your great wonders, Lord—the building of the ark, the flood. Being here is yet another of your great miracles. It's all a bit strange, but also very exciting. I look forward to asking my question in the morning. When you set us some new tasks over the next few days, could you set some sort of building project? I did enjoy making that ark!' The Lord God and Noah laugh together.

'Is there anything else you'd like to know before I let you go?' the Lord God says.

Noah pauses to think and then asks, 'When do we start voting for people to leave?'

'Tomorrow evening,' replies the Lord God. 'If that's all, you may now leave the Holy of Holies.' Noah departs.

The Lord God announces that Joseph is now to go to the Holy of Holies. In reply to the question about how it's going for him, Joseph answers, 'I have always been faithful to you, Lord, even in the worst of times, whether in prison for all those years or sold as a slave. Now you have brought me here, and although it's hard to understand, I accept it. I find it amazing to meet all these people who have heard about me, people from centuries in my future. You ask me how it's going. Well, it's fascinating, although also quite bizarre.'

Moses is next in. The last time Moses spoke to the Lord, his face shone![31] How will he look when he walks out of the Holy of Holies in a few moments? He too tells the Lord God how astonishing it is that they are all there together. He adds that he feels there should be a few more rules and regulations, with appropriate punishments for poor behaviour. The Lord God says that he will think about it, but he also advises Moses to relax a little and stop thinking about laws, day in, day out. Apart from this, Moses has nothing else to say. He is allowed to leave the Holy of Holies.

The next three to go in are Joshua, Rahab and Deborah. They don't have a great deal to say to the Lord God. They too express their surprise and bewilderment at being there.

Next it's Samson's turn to enter the Holy of Holies. 'I have to thank you for bringing me here,' Samson says in response to the opening question. 'I don't know how you did it, but—thanks! The last things I remember from life are having my eyes poked out, being sent to grind at the mill, torture, and finally being led to the two pillars in the Temple of Dagon, which I destroyed. Now I'm here. I can see. There's good food and wine, some pretty women. I'm very happy! There are a few odd types around, but I can cope with that.

'I do love what Ruth said about me yesterday. It's not often that people have spoken about me like that, and it certainly made me stop and think a bit. I know how much I always let you down, Lord, breaking my vows and that, but I do appreciate you bringing me here. I hope some of the others are getting to like me, and that I don't get voted out too soon.'

'If you behave yourself, Samson,' the Lord God replies, 'you may be here longer than you think.'

'Let's hope so,' says Samson. He takes his leave.

After Samson, Ruth pops in and tells the Lord God that all is well with her. Then it's Saul's turn. He walks into the Holy of Holies, looking miserable as usual. When he is seated, the Lord God asks, 'How are you feeling, Saul?'

'Is that supposed to be a joke?' Saul answers sullenly. 'Surely you know I hate being here. It would have been a bit better if David wasn't here as well, but even so, I'm fed up and I want to leave.'

'Things aren't really that bad, are they, Saul?' replies the Lord God. 'You enjoyed hearing David's awful story of adultery and murder and, on the first night here, you enjoyed cutting that piece of material from his robe.'

'I got some satisfaction from those things, I suppose,' says Saul. 'But I'm generally unhappy.'

'Why not try to talk to David?' asks the Lord God. 'If you can try and sort a few things out, perhaps he can start singing and playing to you again. You know how much that used to soothe your dark moods.'

'Listen, Lord!' Saul raises his voice. 'I'm not interested in anything you have to say. I don't want to be here. End of story!' He storms out through the main tent and runs off on his own somewhere. The others can't help noticing this, but choose to ignore him.

Finally it's David's turn to enter the Holy of Holies. The Lord God asks him how he's coping. David explains how awkward it is being there with Saul. He also explains how bad he felt, retelling the story of Bathsheba and Uriah, adding that he still felt a lot of guilt about what he had done.

The Lord God reminds David that he has truly repented and received forgiveness a long time ago, and that that is the end of the matter.

'David,' says the Lord God, 'if I was to ask you just one favour— see if you can do anything to improve relations between you and Saul. I know it will be hard, but would you please try?'

'Of course I will, Lord,' David replies immediately. 'But I don't know what good it will do.'

On that note, he stands up and leaves the Holy of Holies.

After a while, the Lord God makes another announcement to them all. 'I'd like to thank you for coming into the Holy of Holies and sharing some of your thoughts and feelings. Remember, you are free to come and speak to me there whenever you wish.

'I now have a further task for you, and you must all take part. Those who do well may eat and drink in abundance this evening. Those who fail to complete the task adequately will have to go straight to their sleeping quarters, where they will remain until tomorrow morning. They will have a little fruit and water only for the rest of this day.' One or two of the men groan audibly when they hear this.

'Your task will be to perform a mime to the others. It must be about something that happened to you in your lifetime, something quite significant. The others must try to guess what you are acting out. Those of you whose lives came first—like you, Eve, and Noah —will not be able to guess what some of the others are miming, but don't worry about that. The others will be able to guess what you're miming! Just make a good effort, all of you, and you will be rewarded. This task will start in two hours.'

There's a fair bit of discussion between the characters after this announcement. Pretty soon, though, they each go off into a quiet corner to think about what they might perform.

Samson and Noah walk over to the wine and help themselves to generous amounts. They sit together for a while, talking and laughing, their voices gradually getting louder.

The two hours soon pass. The Lord God announces, 'It's time to mime!'

'It's time to mime. What a nice little rhyme!' Samson sings out. Some of the others laugh. Saul just tuts, obviously thinking how pointless the whole exercise is.

The voice of the Lord God fills the air again. 'Gather in the main living and eating area in the tent, please. When you are comfortable, Eve will begin her mime.'

They sit around in a circle, with Eve standing in the middle. Samson suddenly guffaws, 'I hope she mimes the bit where she's naked in the garden of Eden!'

'Don't be so vulgar!' Moses says sternly.

With a bitter smile, Saul says, 'Let's hope she isn't naked. David might not be able to control himself.'

David's furious face shows that he is ready to jump up and punch Saul for that remark, but Deborah manages to calm him down, telling him that Saul is just not worth it.

'You're not funny, you're just a sick man,' Joseph says to Saul coldly. 'What is your problem? Try acting like a king!'

The others murmur agreement. Things eventually calm down again, and Eve begins.

You will not believe what happens next! What Samson hoped for a few moments earlier suddenly becomes reality. In front of them all, in silence, Eve removes her clothing. The others sit there, mouths open in shock. Eve walks around with the most beautiful smile on her face, looking happy and peaceful.

Moses raises his hand to give an answer to the mime. Samson shouts over to him, 'Don't rush, Moses, let's take our time about this!' Noah and Joshua grin. Eventually, Rahab urges Moses to explain what he thinks it's all about.

Moses says solemnly, 'Well, it's an easy one to guess, and a wonderful mime to watch. For a moment I imagined the beauty of the world at the beginning—the wonderful innocence, no sin or shame. Thank you, Eve, for giving us all a glimpse of Paradise.'

'A glimpse of something else, more like!' Samson sniggers.

'Don't spoil things, Samson,' Ruth says. 'There was something so beautiful and innocent about that mime.'

'You guessed correctly, Moses,' Eve replies quietly. 'That's how things were in the beginning, and the way things were meant to be. I'm glad you were able to glimpse that.' She slips back into her clothes and sits down with the others.

'I suppose it's my turn now,' says Noah slowly. He moves to the middle of the circle and, for the next few moments, he simply stands there, making shovelling movements. The others stare at him, confused. Eventually Joseph calls out, 'You're building the ark!'

'No,' replies Noah. 'Keep guessing.' He continues shovelling. In the end, it's David who says, 'We have no idea. Please tell us.'

'Joseph was close when he mentioned the ark.' Noah straightens up and looks round at them all. 'Remember, I had two of every animal in the world on the ark. What I was miming was me shovelling up all the dung they left and dumping it in the sea!'

This has the group in hysterics. Even Saul manages a small smile. Noah sits down, looking quite pleased with himself for managing to entertain the group so well.

Next up is Joseph. He walks into the middle and the first thing he does is lie down on the floor, pretending to go to sleep. After a few seconds, with his eyes still closed, he stands up. He starts to move his hands as if tying something up. He then stands totally straight, and proceeds to walk in a circle, while pointing back to where he had been standing. With his finger still pointing, he bows down. He then moves round a little further and bows again. He does this eleven times. At the end of it all, he lies down again as if asleep. Finally, he stands up and looks at the others. 'That's my mime. What was it?'

The others think for a while. Surprisingly, it's Saul who motions to speak. 'I've heard the stories about you, the little dreamer boy. You must have been a nightmare to have as a brother. From what I understand, you were a thoroughly spoilt brat.'

'Despite thinking that Saul is totally mad,' adds Samson, 'I'm afraid that I have to agree with him here. I heard how you were Daddy's little wonder boy. Just think how bad your brothers must have felt, seeing you being treated as favourite all the time. I would have hated you, I know that for sure.'

Saul continues, 'To make matters even worse, there was the dream you had, the one you have just mimed, where you and your brothers were tying up sheaves of wheat, and your sheaf stood tall and your brothers' sheaves bowed down to yours. They must have been furious when you went round saying that you would rule over them one day. How could you treat them like that?'

'Whatever you might think, Saul,' Moses interrupts, 'Joseph's dreams were from the Lord God. They were dreams that actually did come true. He became second-in-command of Egypt and, as a result, he saved his people from starvation. Surely you know the story?'

'Of course I know the story,' Saul snaps back. 'Those people he saved—their descendants ended up as slaves!'

'Why are you so gloomy, Saul?' asks Rahab, exasperated. 'You look at the negative side of everything. I've never known anyone as miserable as you.'

Samson laughs loudly at this. 'And you're just the opposite, Samson!' Rahab goes on, sounding even more irritated. 'For you, everything is just one big joke!'

'I think we should continue,' says Moses. It is now his turn. Hitching up his robe, he crouches down, and then starts hopping about. The others find this very entertaining. Until now Moses has seemed the most serious among them, and to see him hopping on the ground is funny to say the least. He eventually stops, quite out of breath. David leans over to him, 'I've no idea what that was all about, but could you do it again for us? It was great entertainment!'

Eve, Noah and Joseph obviously have no idea what it was all about, but the others start thinking hard. What on earth can it be? No one can guess. Ruth asks Moses to give them some sort of clue.

'My people were slaves and were suffering terribly,' Moses replies, still breathless. 'The Lord God told me to go to the Pharaoh and ask him to let the Hebrews go.'

'That's right!' adds David. 'The Pharaoh didn't let the people go, and so those ten awful plagues fell on the people of Egypt.'

'And your mime was one of those plagues, wasn't it?' Joshua concludes triumphantly. 'Of course! You were hopping around like a frog. It was the plague of frogs! Those frogs went everywhere, in the Egyptians' beds, ovens, baking-pans and all over the people themselves.'

'What were the other plagues, Moses?' asks Joseph.

'As David said, there were ten plagues,' Moses answers. 'The water turned to blood, and there were swarms of frogs, gnats and flies. Then there was the death of the animals, boils, hail, locusts and darkness. Then came the most awful plague of all, the death of every firstborn son in Egypt, from the Pharaoh's son to the son of a slave girl, and the firstborn of all the cattle as well. It was after this final plague that the Pharaoh let the Lord God's people go.'[32]

'It's amazing,' Joseph says thoughtfully. 'It was Egypt that saved the Lord God's people in my day, and it was Egypt that nearly destroyed them years later.'

Moses goes back to his place. Joshua stands up, ready to begin his mime. Rahab is paying full attention now. She feels quite confident that she will be able to guess what he will do. After all, she was around for a lot of Joshua's lifetime!

Joshua starts by moving forward, but each time he takes a step, something seems to stop him and he has to retreat. He repeats this a few times. Eventually, he pretends to point at some people, motioning them to go in front of him. Then he imitates one of these men, moving his arms as if carrying something. Then he once again moves forward, and this time he is able to continue. After a while he stops. He moves his right arm as if summoning people to follow him.

'I know! I know!' shouts Rahab.

'You're bound to know,' Deborah calls over, with a smile. 'You were there!'

'Too right!' adds Samson. 'Let us lot try to guess first.'

Suddenly, Saul jumps to his feet. 'I've had enough of this stupid game. I want nothing more to do with it!'

They all hear the voice of the Lord God: 'Saul, make your way straight to your sleeping quarters. No meal for you this evening. Take a little water with you, and a few pieces of fruit. Remain there until morning.'

'I'll be glad to!' Saul replies.

The others are speechless. Some of them stare at him, shaking their heads and obviously wondering what on earth is wrong.

'Well, let's get back to Joshua's mime,' says Samson. 'Were you trying to move forward, and finding you couldn't, and so you had to get some others to help you?'

'You're getting there,' Joshua nods.

Rahab clearly knows the answer, but waits to see if anyone else can guess. She eventually gives them a clue. 'If Joshua was camped at Acacia and then had to get to Jericho, what would prevent him from advancing?'

'Why, of course!' exclaims David. 'It's the River Jordan. Not only was the Jordan in front of you, but I believe it was also in flood—impossible to cross.'

'That's right,' adds Rahab. 'The people that Joshua summoned to go ahead of him were the priests carrying the covenant box. As soon as they stepped into the river, it stopped flowing. The priests went to stand in the middle of the river on dry ground, and all the people were able to cross. It was a great miracle.'[33]

'Well, well!' Moses says to Joshua. 'You obviously learned well. I parted the Red Sea, you parted the Jordan…'

'Yeah, and later we can sit outside in the pool. Maybe, together, you can part that!' interrupts Samson. They all laugh.

When it comes to Rahab's turn, she admits that she has no idea what to do. The others try to encourage her, but she seems a little uncomfortable about the whole exercise. Maybe she is afraid of some nasty comment from Samson about her past. Whatever the reason, she refuses to take part. The Lord God orders her to her sleeping quarters. Deborah clearly feels sorry for Rahab, because she too declines to mime, and also ends up in the sleeping area with a bit of water and fruit by way of an evening meal.

Next up is Samson. He immediately walks to the middle, bends down as if to pick something up from the floor, and then starts to mime fighting, which is quite awesome to watch! So far, Samson has come across as a joker but, for the first time, the others see him as a fierce, frightening warrior.

Ruth and David are the only ones left who might have any idea what he is doing. They exchange glances and then both start singing, 'With the jawbone of a donkey I killed a thousand men; with the jawbone of a donkey I piled them up in piles.'[34]

'The thing you picked up from the floor,' says David, 'was the jawbone of an ass. Everyone knows that great story about how you killed a thousand Philistine men with only the jawbone as a weapon, at Ramath Lehi.'

'I always imagined the Philistine commander having to go back to his king and explain,' adds Ruth. 'I pictured him telling the king that he had thousands of men, hundreds of chariots, the most advanced weapons around. Then the king would ask, "And what weapons did Samson have?" "The jawbone of an ass!" the commander would reply!'

The others join in her laughter as they picture the scene.

Then Ruth steps up to begin her mime, although it's doubtful that anyone except David will know what she is doing. She walks over to David and lies down at his feet, pretending to sleep. Then she wakes up, takes off her cloak and spreads it out on the floor. She then mimes filling her cloak with something. She picks it up, although it is apparently now very heavy, and announces that that is the end of her mime.

Joseph raises his hand immediately to give the answer.

'How on earth can you know what she was miming?' asks Noah.

'It was revealed to me in a dream last night,' Joseph replies.

'You and your dreams!' Samson rolls his eyes.

'I certainly know what Ruth was miming,' says David, 'but tell us about your dream, Joseph. Let's see if you really do have some sort of gift as far as dreams are concerned!'

'I will tell you my dream,' Joseph replies. 'I dreamed that Naomi was telling Ruth that she was going to find a husband for her. In my dream I saw Ruth dressed in her best clothes, and I saw her putting on make-up. She looked quite beautiful.'

'And exactly what sort of dream did you have?' asks Samson, with a knowing leer.

Joseph ignores Samson and continues. 'Naomi tells Ruth to wait until Boaz is asleep, and to go and lift up his covers and lie at his feet. This she does, and that's what we all saw in Ruth's mime.

'During the night, Boaz wakes up and is quite shocked to find Ruth lying at his feet. After he finds out who she is, Ruth asks him to marry her, as he is a close relative. Boaz is extremely impressed by her family loyalty. He allows her to stay at his feet until just before daybreak. He then fills her cloak with 20 kilogrammes of barley. This we also saw in Ruth's mime. In short, they eventually get married.'

Ruth and David are astonished at his insight.

'That's even more detail than I know,' says David, amazed at the accuracy of Joseph's dream.

'You have described my mime perfectly, Joseph,' Ruth smiles, and sits down.

Just before David stands up to perform the final mime, Joseph leans forward. 'I don't mean to upset anyone, but I also had a dream about what David is about to do.'

'No wonder your brothers thought you were a real pain,' Joshua snorts.

'The Lord God gives me the dreams,' says Joseph simply. 'I just tell people about them.'

'I could just sit here and do nothing,' David retorts. 'Then your dream won't come true.'

'But maybe that's what I dreamed you would do!' Joseph laughs.

'How can I win?' David laughs with him. 'Here's my mime.' He stands still for a moment, and then looks up, as if at something huge. He starts pointing at whatever he is looking at, and pretends to shout. Next, he takes an imaginary object from his belt, bends down and picks up something from the floor. He puts it into the object he took from his belt.

David looks up again, and points as if aiming with his left hand. With his right hand he starts to swing the imaginary object around his head extremely fast. After a few seconds, he suddenly lets something fly from his right hand towards the tall person or object he is looking at.

Whatever that object is now seems to fall to the floor. David walks over to where it is lying, picks up a large weapon of some kind and lifts it above his head with an effort. Then, with one mighty movement, he brings the weapon down in a chopping motion, and stands back, looking at the others.

'I reckon there's a sling and a sword involved,' says Samson. 'I recognize fighting when I see it. I hope it was some Philistine scum you were giving a good hiding to!'

'You're quite close, Samson,' David replies. 'Well done! Perhaps we can ask the dreamer over there to fill in the details, as he reckons he saw the whole thing in his sleep last night.'

Joseph frowns and reiterates the fact that all his dreams and ability to interpret come from the Lord God. David tells him that he is only teasing, and asks him to explain the mime in a little more detail, if he can.

Joseph tells them his dream. 'I saw a huge giant of a man. His name was Goliath, and he was twice or three times the size of Samson. He threatened to make all the Israelites slaves, and he was asking the Israelites to send a man to fight him. For 40 days he challenged them, but they were all too terrified to fight.

'In my dream, I saw David as a young boy. He told King Saul that he would fight Goliath. The whole court laughed at him, but David told the king that as a shepherd he had killed bears and lions, and he would do the same with this evil Goliath.'

'Nice one, David!' says Samson. 'Wish I had been around at the same time. Together we could have wiped the Philistine heathen off the face of the earth.'

Joseph continues, 'In the end, Saul sensed that David possessed some inner strength of spirit, and agreed to let him fight. He wanted David to wear his armour, but it was far too big and David looked ridiculous in it. In my dream, David said that he didn't need any armour as he was going out to attack and not to defend himself.'

'That's the spirit!' breaks in Noah, clenching a fist.

'When David went out to face Goliath,' Joseph goes on, 'his words were magnificent. He was a young lad with amazing faith in the Lord God. He walked up to the giant and said, "You come against me with a sword, spear and javelin, but I come against you in the name of the Lord Almighty, the God of the Israelite army, which you have defied. Today you will be defeated. I will cut off your head, and the bodies of the Philistines will be given to the birds and beasts. Then the whole world will know that Israel has a God, and that he does not need swords and spears to save his people."

'The rest of the mime you can now work out.' David defeats Goliath with nothing but a sling. The stone hits Goliath in the forehead, killing him almost immediately. David then chops off the giant's head.'[35]

'Magnificent!' Moses cries out.

'I was quite shocked at the Bathsheba story,' says Eve, 'but this was a wonderful story of faith, bravery and trust in the Lord God.'

'Your dream is once again totally accurate,' David tells Joseph. 'As far as the courage and real faith are concerned, I don't really know about that.'

'And you're modest as well!' Eve smiles.

The voice of the Lord God interrupts their conversation. 'Excellent! As promised, you will be rewarded with a good meal this evening, and some fine wine. The others, sadly, must stay confined to their sleeping quarters.'

An instant later, the table behind them is filled with all kinds of wonderful food. There is roast lamb and goat, choice fowl, and fish, much of it cooked with onions and garlic. There is also plenty of bread and fruit, and quite a few skinfuls of wine.

They are delighted at this glorious banquet. Moses collects a jug of water, and goes round to each of the others, pouring out a little water so that they can wash their hands. They gather round the table, and it is Samson who lifts his arms and says, 'Blessed are you, Lord God, King of the world, who brings us bread from the earth.'

They sit down and enjoy the feast. At one point, Saul sticks his head out of the men's sleeping quarters and asks them to keep the noise down. Samson shouts back, 'If you weren't so miserable, you could have been here with us.'

The conversation is good at the meal. They share with each other many of their life experiences. There is plenty of laughter, and they certainly enjoy the fine wine. In fact, Noah gets quite drunk. Joseph tells the others about how Noah once got drunk and removed all his clothes and lay naked in his tent.[36]

'What a terrible thought!' says Samson, grinning. 'Let's get him to bed now before he strips off!' He and Joseph manage to drag Noah out to his bed. He falls into a deep sleep almost immediately.

After a while, a few of the others feel a little tired and tipsy and make their way to bed too. As usual, Samson is the last one left. He wanders outside (staggering, to be precise) with a skinful of wine, sits down by his favourite tree, singing to himself, and eventually falls asleep.

DAY FOUR

The following morning, a little later than usual, the voice of the Lord God announces loudly that it is time to get up. Rahab, Deborah and Saul are already up, not surprisingly after such an early night. They have already found some bread and fruit to eat.

The others eventually make it to the breakfast table, including Noah, who looks quite rough. Somehow or other, Samson is as bright and chirpy as ever, despite sleeping outside all night and drinking a fair amount of wine.

Breakfast is a quiet affair, with a few grunts and moans coming from some of the characters, especially Noah! When the meal is over, the Lord God declares, 'You may all rest for a further hour. I then want you to go to the communal pool, where you will continue the question-and-answer task. When this is over, you will each report to the Holy of Holies and vote for the person who you think should leave today, telling me in one sentence why they should go.'

Who will be leaving the Lord God's compound today? Do some folk still think deep down that Eve should go? She was the one who brought sin into the world. Maybe some are still shocked at David's story of adultery and murder! Is Saul making everyone miserable? Why is Rahab here, anyway? Wasn't she just a prostitute? These are some of the questions that the characters are asking themselves. We will have to wait and see what happens!

The hour soon passes, and they all take their places outside. Today is the hottest day yet, so they are pleased to be in the cool and shady pool. Everyone looks at Joshua, as it is he who has to ask the first question. He directs it at Deborah. 'I led the people into the land of Canaan, and I've learned that you, like Samson, became one of the judges to lead and rule Israel. Could you tell me a little about yourself—what you did and what you achieved?'

Deborah gives Joshua a wry look. 'What probably shocks many of you, first of all, is that as a woman I was actually a leader of Israel.'

'You were more than that,' David interrupts. 'From what I understand from history, you were quite unique. You were a prophetess, a judge and a military leader all in one. That was a powerful combination of authority and responsibility held by only two other Israelites that I know of, and they were Moses and Samuel. Moses, of course, you all know. Samuel was the prophet, judge and military leader who appointed Saul and me as kings, because the people of Israel wanted a king like other nations.'

Deborah continues, 'I didn't realize there was anything unique about me, but thank you, David. I was the leader of the nation. I helped settle their disputes and, as a prophetess, I helped give the nation direction from God. As someone called by God, I think I earned the respect of the people. An example of this respect was when I commanded Barak, the commander of the Israelite army, to attack Sisera, the commander of the enemy forces of that time. Barak was too afraid to do it and insisted that I come with him. He told me that my presence would guarantee victory. This showed the level of confidence that Israel seemed to have in me.

'I told Barak that I would go with him but, because he didn't have the faith simply to carry out my order, I told him that he would get no credit for the victory. I told him that Sisera would be handed over to a woman.'

'And what a great story that is!' shouts Samson. 'A woman called Jael drove a tent peg right through Sisera's head! Good effort!'[37]

A few of them flinch at the thought! Joshua thanks Deborah for her answer.

Next, it's Rahab's turn to ask a question. She begins, 'My question is for any of you who may wish to answer. I get the feeling that some of you here know me as no more that Rahab the prostitute. Is that how you see me? Do some of you even wonder what I'm doing here?'

By the silly look on Samson's face, they can tell that he is about to come out with some ridiculous comment. For once, though, he holds back, somehow sensing that it might just be inappropriate.

Joshua immediately explains how Rahab played a vital role in the capture and destruction of Jericho, and in no way does he see her as 'the prostitute'. It's David who speaks up for her next.

'I can tell everyone here that Rahab has always been seen as an example of active faith and, despite her past before she turned to the true God, she was later considered among the righteous. It was by faith that the people were able to cross the Red Sea as if on dry land—but when the Egyptians tried to do the same, they were drowned. By faith the walls of Jericho fell down after the Israelites had marched round them for seven days. By faith Rahab the prostitute was not killed with those who had disobeyed God, because she had given friendly welcome to the spies.[38] That's how I see it. There's one other wonderful thing you need to know, Rahab, and Ruth knows what I'm talking about. We were going to tell you, anyway.'

Rahab looks most intrigued. David continues, 'As you know, you went on to marry Salmon, an Israelite. You gave birth to Boaz. Boaz married Ruth and they had Obed. Obed was the father of Jesse, and of course Jesse was my father.'

Rahab bursts into tears. David and Ruth both go over and embrace her for a long time. It's an emotional moment, and many of the others are visibly moved by the events unfolding before them. For once, even Samson and Saul stay quiet and, in their own ways, seem touched by what's going on.

This has been a perfect response to Rahab's question. David and Ruth stay sitting next to her—it will take her quite a while to get used to this new knowledge!

The next question is from Deborah, and she directs it at Moses. 'Moses, you were the great leader of Israel during the exodus from Egypt. The one great lesson I was always taught about you was the example of your tenacious faith in the Lord God. All those around you continually doubted you and the Lord God, and they were always rebelling, but you strongly believed in what God was doing.

'What I don't understand, though, is that despite this amazing faith that you showed throughout your life, you couldn't enter the promised land. Why was that? You of all people deserved to do so. I was taught that, somehow or other, you disobeyed God and your punishment was to be barred from entering Canaan. What did you do to disobey God?'

A few of the others agree that they have never fully understood what Moses had done wrong.

Moses proceeds to explain. 'Many people at the time also found it difficult to understand why I had been punished by being barred from the promised land. But I understood why. We were camped at Kidesh in the wilderness of Zin. There was no water where we camped and, as ever, the people came running up to Aaron and me and complained bitterly. They moaned about having no water, no food, and that they were going to die. I looked up into the heavens. A dazzling light appeared before me, and I heard the Lord God say to me, "Take the stick that's in front of the covenant box, and call the whole community together. In front of them all, I want you to speak to that rock over there, and then water will come gushing out. The people and animals will then be able to drink."[39]

'I did what the Lord God told me to do, but when I went to the rock I screamed at the people. I was furious with them and the way they were always complaining and moaning. I called them rebels. I was so angry that, instead of speaking to the rock, I smashed it twice with my stick. The Lord God was furious with me. He said to me, "Because you didn't have enough faith to acknowledge my holy power before the people, you will not lead them into the land that I have promised to give them."'[40]

'Is that all you did wrong?' Samson asks. 'I did terrible things in my life, and so have some of the others, from what I've been hearing. You got a little angry with the people—and quite rightly so —yet the Lord God bans you from the promised land. Charming!'

'You don't really understand, Samson,' Moses answers patiently. 'Many times in my life, the Lord God had gone to great lengths to demonstrate to his people his mastery over nature. This terrible crisis in the desert was another opportunity for him to show that control. If I had simply followed his instructions, the people would have had further proof of his unfailing providence, and in this case it would have been a miracle right on time! But I failed the Lord God. I used the situation to shout and scream and condemn the people. I demonstrated nothing but anger and sarcasm. I even smashed the rock twice in anger. This occasion should have been a joyful manifestation of God's power, but I turned it into one of bitterness and denunciation. In short, I failed to glorify the Lord God before the people. It was a terrible thing that I did, and I fully deserved my punishment.'

'What you say does make sense,' Ruth comments, 'but your anger at the time is quite understandable. The Lord God performed one amazing miracle after another during those years, but still the people complained!'

Deborah thanks Moses for his answer to her question.

Next up is the giant Samson. What on earth is he going to ask? Everyone stares at him expectantly. Samson looks round, smiling. 'I want you all to pretend that we decide to escape from here. We have all had action-packed lives, full of adventure. It would really interest me to know how each of you, with all your experiences, would plan an escape from this place. That's my question. How would you escape? Keep your answers short, and we'll go in order, starting with Eve.'

'That's simple,' Eve replies. 'I would just do something that the Lord God has forbidden, and then we would be thrown out!' The others find this hilarious.

Next comes Noah. 'Well, there are plenty of trees around here. I know how to build boats.' He shows them a little wooden boat that he has been carving over the last couple of days. They are all impressed. 'You know about the ark. I would get us to build a huge boat. Then we would pray hard for a lot of rain, and we would just float over the walls!'

The others like this answer as well. Samson's question is proving to be an entertaining one.

Joseph says, 'I can't give you the exact plan at the moment, because I need to dream one up first!' Again, the others love it. Joseph goes on to explain that he'd need to go to bed with the problem on his mind first, and then the answer would come to him in his sleep. The others ask him to share any good dreams that do come along about how to escape, and Joseph agrees with a smile.

Now it is the turn of Moses to describe his plan. 'If I can part the Red Sea, I'm pretty sure I can part those walls!'

'Good answer,' nods Samson. 'Now it's you, Joshua, and I think we know what you're going to say.' The others laugh.

'Yes, you've guessed it,' says Joshua. 'We'll get those walls tumbling down! We'll march round once a day for six days, in silence. On the seventh day, we'll march around seven times. Then we will shout with all our might and the walls will come tumbling down.'

'Nice plan,' Samson grins, 'but I don't know if I could wait seven days!'

Rahab gives her answer: 'I'll stick with Joshua's plan, if you don't mind. I've seen it work before, and I'm sure it would work again!'

'A good reply!' Samson is delighted at the responses to his question.

Then it's Deborah's turn. 'I would not think about any escape plan unless it was the Lord God's will.' This is not quite the answer that Samson is expecting, but he says nothing and turns to ask Ruth what her plan would be.

'As you all know, I have had no military experience in my life,' Ruth replies shyly. 'I've found your answers so far very interesting. I know it's only a pretence, but I'd go along with any of the plans so far—but perhaps not Eve's, which involves disobeying the Lord God. I could never do that, although I know you were only joking, Eve.'

'An honest answer,' says Samson. 'Thanks for that. Now over to Mr Happy himself, Saul.'

Saul is not amused with Samson's witty remark. He says sarcastically, 'There would be no point in me coming up with any plan, as it would be bound to fail!'

David suddenly remembers that the Lord God has asked him to try to get on with Saul, so he speaks up. 'That's nonsense, Saul.'

Saul looks round at David, shocked. David continues, 'One of the greatest military plans I ever heard was how Saul defeated King Nahash of Ammon. None of you will know this story, but Nahash besieged the town of Jabesh in Gilead. He wanted to poke out the right eye of everyone in the town and bring disgrace on the whole of Israel.'

The others are shocked to hear of this episode. Many of them clench their fists, as if they would have loved to get their hands on that cruel king. David goes on, 'The leaders of Jabesh sent messengers to Saul, asking for help. I have to tell you that Saul was a real hero. When the messengers got to him, he was just returning from the field with his oxen. When he heard the news, he chopped his oxen into pieces. He sent the messengers to carry the pieces throughout the land of Israel with this warning: "Whoever does not follow Saul and Samuel into battle will have this done to his oxen!"'

'Good effort!' shouts Samson.

'In short, Saul managed to gather 330,000 men,' David continues. 'They slaughtered the Ammonites. Saul won a famous victory and all the people celebrated.'[41]

Everyone congratulates Saul, clapping and smiling.

Saul turns to David and thanks him, his voice suddenly trembling with emotion. 'So you do respect me! Maybe you are a good man after all. I've just been so tormented by jealousy, and imprisoned by these dark moods, that I can only think about myself and my own feelings.'

The others cheer even more. Could this be the beginning of the breakthrough that they have been waiting for? David tells Saul that he will happily play music and sing to help him out of his depression. Saul looks grateful, and tentatively pats David on the shoulder.

Then the Lord God makes an announcement. 'Well done to you all so far. I have heard some good questions. I'm glad to see Saul looking happier. There are still a few questions that need to be asked, and I want those to be done tomorrow morning. I've decided that you may have a few hours' break. After that, it will be time to vote for one person to leave the tent. One by one you will come into the Holy of Holies and say who you want to leave and why.'

Everyone is quiet for a while after this. The only event of note during the next few hours is that David enters the Holy of Holies and asks the Lord God if he can have a small harp. He explains that relations with Saul have begun to thaw, and playing a harp would enable him to help Saul fight his dark moods. The Lord God agrees to this request.

At last it is time to vote. Eve is summoned to the Holy of Holies first. 'Whom are you voting to leave and why?' the Lord God asks her.

'I am voting for Saul to leave. He has spoken unkindly to me, and he is always miserable and making others feel down.' Eve speaks quietly but firmly.

'Thank you for your decision,' says the Lord God.

Next is Noah. 'I vote for Eve to leave. There is no excuse for what she did in the Garden of Eden.'

The Lord God summons Joseph, who explains that he was going to vote for Saul, but Saul seems to be improving a little. On balance he votes for Deborah, because she didn't take part in the mime task and he finds her a little stern.

Moses also votes for Deborah, giving the same reasons as Joseph.

Joshua votes for Saul, explaining that he finds him far too miserable.

Rahab votes for David. Her reason for doing so is that she is still shocked by the story of his adultery and Uriah's murder.

Deborah votes for Samson. She says that Samson takes nothing seriously, and she can't understand why he is there in the first place.

Samson, like Joseph, says that he was going to vote for Saul, but now he will give him a chance, as his mood appears to be lifting. Instead he votes for Deborah to leave. He says that he finds her boring, and she is the ugliest of all the women there!

Ruth votes for David, even though she is his great-grandmother. She is also still shocked at his awful behaviour with Bathsheba and her husband.

Saul votes for Samson. Until today, it was quite likely that he would have voted for David, but Saul doesn't like Samson's continual jibes and ridiculous humour.

Finally it's David's turn to vote. He says to the Lord God, 'I would like Moses to leave. I find him stern and only concerned about keeping the rules.'

The Lord God summons them to the main communal area of the tent, where they sit in a circle, and announces, 'A decision has been made.' There is a pause. Everybody looks anxious. The first person to leave my tent is...' There is another pause. The atmosphere is electric, but the Lord God keeps them waiting for a few more seconds.

'Come on!' a couple of them murmur.

'Deborah!' announces the Lord God. 'You have been chosen to leave the tent. Please be ready to go in a few minutes.'

Most of the others look shocked. The women immediately gather round Deborah and hug her, but she doesn't really show any emotion. She tells them all how much she has enjoyed meeting them.

With the time up, the Lord God asks Deborah to make her way to the large gate built in the wall. The rest walk over there with her. The huge gate swings open. On the other side there is just a dazzling light. Deborah says a final goodbye, and this time, there are tears in her eyes. She walks through the gate into the light and disappears. Where she has gone, no one knows—no one, that is, except the Lord God. The rest of the characters walk back to the main tent in silence, although Samson stays by the wall, on the lookout for more honey.

Surprisingly, Saul says to David just then, 'Hey, David, we're all feeling a little strange now that Deborah has had to leave. How about you play the harp and sing us something to cheer us up?'

'Great idea!' agrees Joseph.

Rahab suggests that they go and sit around the pool, drink some wine, eat some bread and listen to David's music. There is general agreement and David goes to collect his harp.

When everyone's settled with a glass of wine in their hand, David prepares to sing his first song. Then suddenly he looks up to the sky and calls out, 'Lord God, can you hear me?'

'I can hear you!' the voice of the Lord God replies.

David continues, 'I was wondering whether you could provide me with some trumpets, lyres, drums, cymbals and flutes?' Before he has even finished asking, the pool is surrounded with everything he has asked for.

David explains to the others, 'Right, I'm going to sing and play you one of my favourite songs. It's a song of praise to the Lord God, and many of the words refer to musical instruments. When you get used to the song, I would like you to take an instrument and join me in praising the Lord God. It doesn't matter whether you can play at all, just take hold of something and make a joyful noise.'

By this time, Samson has returned from his honey session. He is already making his way towards a huge set of cymbals!

'That's the way, Samson,' says David. 'Everyone follow his example.' They all choose an instrument. Now David begins.

Praise God in his temple!
Praise his strength in heaven!
Praise him for all the wonderful things he has done!
Praise his greatness.
Praise him with the trumpets.
Praise him with harps and lyres.
Praise him with drums and dancing.
Praise him with harps and flutes.
Praise him with cymbals, yes praise him with loud cymbals.
Praise God, all living things.
Praise the Lord God![42]

David sings the song through a few times. It has a great rhythm and the others really like it. When they are familiar with the melody, he explains where they should come in with their instruments.

He starts the song again. This time, when he reaches the line about the trumpets, Joseph starts blowing the one that he has grabbed. It is a terrible noise—but a joyful one! Rahab joins in, making a lovely sound on the harp. A few of the others start drumming. Eve, Ruth and Noah begin dancing. When they come to the line 'praise him with loud cymbals', Samson makes the biggest noise yet. As the others roar with laughter, he continues bashing away. It is wonderful fun, as well as truly expressing joy and praise to the Lord God.

At the end they applaud each other and thank David for his skill in leading them.

When they have calmed down, Eve suggests that it is time to prepare a meal. Noah and Joseph go to slaughter an animal. Eve and Ruth collect some vegetables and start work on the cooking. Samson walks over to David and slaps him on the back, thanking him for the great music. They both sit down and start chatting together. Out of the blue, Samson asks, 'Who do you think is the prettiest woman here?'

'I can't answer that!' replies David. 'The Lord God can obviously hear our conversation, so I'm not going to answer you.'

'It's an innocent enough question!' Samson raises his bushy eyebrows. 'I'm sure the Lord God won't mind us simply discussing which is the most beautiful of his female creations here.'

'Well,' says David, 'if you put it like that, I suppose there is no harm in it. But remember the story I told you about Bathsheba! I don't want to get in any trouble like that again. That all started when I just happened to glance at a beautiful woman.'

'Just tell me who you think is the prettiest woman here!' Samson is now really intrigued as to what David will say.

David looks him in the eyes and says, 'Without a shadow of doubt, it has got to be Eve. She is just perfect!'

'Exactly what I think!' shouts Samson. 'Maybe it's because she was the first woman created that she looks so perfect. Just look at those eyes, and that beautiful, flowing black hair, and the wonderful size and shape of her b—'

'That'll do!' interrupts David. 'She is a perfect woman. Let's leave it at that.'

'Why should we leave it at that?' Samson sounds quite annoyed. 'I'm a man, she's a woman, and I think she's beautiful.'

'So what do you intend to do about it?' asks David.

'None of us really knows why we are here,' Samson answers. 'How do we know what we can or can't do? I really like Eve, so I'm going to tell her and see what happens. If the Lord God doesn't like it, I'm sure he'll let me know!'

'I'm sure Eve will let you know if she doesn't like you as well,' David chuckles. 'After all, you were quite unkind to her. I hope you have more luck with her than you did with Delilah!'

'Don't mention that name to me!' Samson spits out. He gets up, looks around for Eve and eventually finds her outside, milking a goat. He walks over and asks her if she would like some help. When Eve says that she would, Samson blurts out, 'You are a very beautiful woman, Eve, perhaps the most beautiful woman I have ever seen.'

Eve stops what she's doing and stares at Samson. She suddenly bursts into laughter. 'Oh Samson, Samson, I'm sure you say that to all the women!' She carries on milking.

'I've called women beautiful before, yes,' says Samson, 'but I've never said to a woman that she is the most beautiful woman I have ever seen. Maybe it's because you were the woman created for Paradise that you're so perfect.'

'Are you sure you haven't been at the wine?' asks Eve jokingly.

She finishes milking and returns to the main tent. Samson follows her. Eve joins the other women in the cooking area and whispers something to them. They all giggle. Samson watches what is going on and guesses that he's the source of their amusement. He stalks back to David.

'Well, how did it go, big man?' asks David.

'She doesn't believe a word I'm saying,' answers Samson gloomily. 'She seems to think I'm just joking.'

'Well, you are the one who generally acts the clown around here,' says David with a smile. 'It's not surprising that she doesn't take you seriously. If I was you, I'd just forget about it. Who knows—you or she might even be voted out tomorrow. Just enjoy yourself!'

'That's what I was trying to do,' Samson groans. 'I wanted to enjoy myself with a beautiful woman!' He stomps out of the tent looking more than a little frustrated. David shakes his head, finding the whole episode merely amusing.

After an hour or so, it's time to eat. A sheep has been slaughtered, the blood drained and the meat roasted. The women have made a lentil-based stew. Everybody washes their hands, Eve says the blessing, and they tuck in to the fine meal.

While they are eating, Joseph wonders aloud whether they should ask the Lord God if they could carry on with their questions now, rather than waiting until tomorrow morning. Everyone agrees with him.

Joseph shouts out, 'Lord God, can you hear me?'

'I hear everything!' is the Lord God's response. 'And I know what you wish to ask. The answer is yes. You may continue your questions now, during the meal. I believe that it's Ruth's turn.'

'Give me a few minutes, and then I'll ask my question,' Ruth responds.

'Who's for more wine?' asks Samson. A few people hold up their glasses and Samson fills them. After a while, Ruth announces that she is ready. The others look at her expectantly, keen to hear what she will ask.

Ruth turns to David. 'Dear great-grandson, I hope you don't mind, but I would like to bring up the Bathsheba episode again. I know it's painful to talk about, but I would like to know more about the Lord God's condemnation of the affair and your repentance. Could you tell us exactly what happened to lead to your repentance? I only ask because I would really like to know what sort of person you are, and I feel sure you are a good man.'

The faces of the others show how they feel for David. It must be so difficult discussing a personal sin in front of them all. Slowly, David begins his answer. 'I described my evil deed the other day. I committed a terrible sin, and I thought I had formed an effective cover-up plan. But I overlooked one small detail: none of us can hide our hearts from the Lord God.'

'You can say that again!' Samson chips in.

'I heard that!' booms the voice of the Lord God.

'See what I mean?' Samson exclaims ruefully.

They all laugh. David continues, 'It was Nathan the prophet who pointed out the error of my ways.'

'I bet he had a right go at you,' says Samson.

'Well no, he didn't. He dealt with the whole incident quite cleverly. He came to see me and told me a parable.'

'Tell us the parable, David,' says Joseph. 'I love a good story.'

'Nathan began by telling me that there were two men living in a city. One was rich, the other poor. He told me that the rich man had a great many flocks and herds. The poor man had nothing except one little ewe lamb. He had bought this little lamb himself, and he nourished it and cared for it. The lamb grew up with him and his children. It would eat his bread and drink from his cup and sleep in his lap. That little lamb was like a daughter to him.'

'I think I'm going to cry,' says Samson with a wink.

'Be quiet!' Eve snaps at him.

David continues. 'A traveller came to visit the rich man. The rich man was so tight-fisted that he didn't kill one of his own animals to feed the traveller. What he did was to take the poor man's lamb and prepare it for his visitor. When Nathan told me this story, I was furious. I told Nathan that the man who did this must die, because it was such an evil thing to do. What Nathan said next nearly destroyed me there and then. He said to me, "You are the man!"'

'Very clever!' says Moses. 'Nathan's parable was a close parallel to what you had done and tried to cover up so skilfully.'

'I guess that shows us that no matter how hard we try, we can't hide from God,' adds Rahab. 'It's best just to be honest with the Lord God. It's not as if he doesn't already know.'

'Nathan really set you up good and proper, and you took the bait.' Samson is very impressed by the whole episode. 'It's interesting, David, that when you passed judgment on the rich man, you were pronouncing judgment on yourself—death! It reminds me that the Lord God is bigger and smarter than we are.'

'The only thing I could say to Nathan was, "I have sinned against the Lord,"' admits David.

'Well done!' Moses shows his approval by nodding vigorously. 'You could have continued in denial, saying "I did not have sex with that woman!" You made no excuses, and you expected to die for what you had done. Through your honesty with the Lord God, you discovered his mercy and grace.'

Surprisingly, Saul then speaks up. 'Well done, David. I was a man who always made excuses to the Lord God. You made a mistake, but you truly are an honest and good man. I always knew that, but I was blinded by my own jealousy.'

You can see from David's face that he really appreciates this comment from Saul. David carries on with his story. 'After my confession to the Lord God, in fact, every morning after that moment, I used to open my eyes and realize that I was alive because of one thing and one thing only—it was by the sheer grace of God. My life changed. My relationship with the Lord God was deepened. It was wonderful. I don't know whether you would be interested, but I wrote a song after this incident. It was like a prayer of repentance. I wasn't just trying to say sorry, I was making a heartfelt plea for forgiveness. I truly wanted to be healed and restored. Would you like me to sing you this song now?'

'What a daft question!' says Samson. 'We'd love to hear it!'

'Here, here!' adds Saul. David gets up to fetch his harp. When he returns, they all fall silent. He tells them that he will sing only part of the song, as it's quite long. He begins:

Be merciful to me, O God,
because of your everlasting love.
Because of your great mercy wipe away my sins!
Wash away all my evil and cleanse me from my sin.

I recognize all my faults;
I am always conscious of my sins.
I have sinned against you, you only.
You are right in judging me, you are right to condemn me.
I have been evil from the day I was born…

It is truth that you require;
Fill my mind with your wisdom…

Let me hear the sounds of joy and gladness;
And though you have crushed and broken me,
I will be happy once again.
Close your eyes to my sins and wipe out all my evil…

Give me again the joy that comes from your salvation,
And make me willing to obey you.[43]

When David finishes, there isn't a dry eye at the table. The song was beautiful. Ruth moves over to David and gives him a huge hug. She certainly seems very happy with how he has answered her question.

After a while, Saul mentions that it is now his turn to ask a question. He stands up. 'My question is simple and it's addressed to David.' He turns to David. 'Because of all the wrongs that I have committed against you, I'd like to ask you one thing. Can you ever forgive me?'

Everyone is amazed. What a change they are witnessing in Saul's character! David says nothing in reply but leaves his place and hugs Saul, kissing him on both cheeks. 'With all the talk about repentance and forgiveness,' he says, 'how could I not forgive you?'

'It was my own fault that my life was such a mess,' Saul mutters. 'I failed to repent sincerely of my sin of disobedience. As a result, the Lord God withdrew his Spirit from me, and I lived out the rest of my days in misery and torment, taking it all out on you.' He begins to cry. Some of the others draw near to hug him as well. Everyone is beginning to feel warmly towards him.

Samson calls out, 'I like all this hugging going on. Eve! Do you fancy a nice big hug?'

'Only in your dreams!' she replies, and everyone laughs. They start to take their places again as Noah says, 'I believe there's just one question left. Over to you, David.'

David addresses the whole table. 'My question is: how would you all like to take up your instruments again, and I'll sing a few songs and we'll make lots of noise and have a party?'

'Brilliant idea!' yells Samson. He loved making a real racket the last time David sang. The others also look excited at the prospect of more music.

For the next hour or so, David sings and plays his harp. The others join in, dancing and making a joyful noise with all the instruments.

A bit later in the evening, when the music-making is finally winding down, the Lord God makes an announcement.

'I have two things to tell you. First of all, I would like to remind you that tomorrow morning you must decide on the next person to leave the tent. Secondly, I'm now going to set you a task, which you will begin immediately.'

'Oh no!' Samson groans.

'You will start first, Samson!' The voice of the Lord God grows louder. 'Your task, everybody, is to weave a piece of cloth.'

'That sounds easy enough,' remarks Joseph.

'I haven't finished yet,' says the Lord God. 'Your task will be to weave a piece of cloth non-stop for the next twelve hours. You will work in pairs. Each pair must weave for at least two hours at a time. For those of you who can't weave, one of you can explain it to the others. You will find a loom outside and you will begin in one hour. First of all, you will need to watch and learn the technique, and then choose your partner. Who will demonstrate using the loom?' Ruth immediately volunteers to do this, and Joseph offers to carry the loom inside.

'Just when I was looking for a good night's sleep,' sighs Moses.

'Now, now! Don't complain,' says David. 'You didn't like it when your people continually complained, did you?'

'That was different,' Moses replies unsmilingly. Some of the others laugh. Joseph returns with the loom and plenty of yarn. Ruth asks the others to gather round so that she can begin her demonstration.

'I should be out hunting lions,' growls Samson, 'not standing here learning how to weave.'

'I know why you don't like weaving,' Saul says slyly. 'Didn't that Delilah of yours once tie some of your hair into her loom so that she could capture you?'

'I smashed up her loom, and I'll do the same to this one if anyone mentions that name again.' Samson pounds the loom with a fist.

'Let's just get on with the demonstration,' says Joseph, trying to calm the situation. Ruth begins. She weaves neatly and quickly, making it look quite easy. Nevertheless, Noah also starts complaining about the task. He mumbles about how he doesn't mind building boats, but why should he be weaving cloth? Some of the others chuckle when they hear this. It seems that quite a few of the men aren't too keen on taking part in this activity—but they have no choice. The group start discussing who will pair up with whom.

'The Lord God announced that Samson has to begin, so who will be his partner?' says Moses. Ruth offers to pair up with Samson and Samson looks happy enough with this arrangement, probably because Ruth is clearly a weaving expert!

'We'll get started now,' Samson announces. 'The rest of you decide who's going to take over in two hours' time.'

The others pair off—Eve and Noah, Joshua and Rahab, Joseph and Moses, and Saul and David (which is good to see). Saul and David agree to take over from Ruth and Samson when the first weaving session is finished.

As it is getting fairly late, and they are starting to feel sleepy after the food, wine and singing, the others decide to go to bed. Samson promises to wake Saul and David when it's their turn, and they all exchange good nights.

Samson and Ruth begin their weaving, and Samson is quite

clumsy at first. As Ruth weaves in one direction, Samson takes the stick and weaves back in the other direction. After a shaky start, though, he soon gets the hang of it and it's not long before they have woven a small section of cloth. From time to time, they exchange a few comments. When an hour or so has passed, Samson decides that he fancies another glass of wine. He offers Ruth some and she accepts graciously. They continue weaving, chatting and sipping their wine.

A little later—and maybe it is the wine talking—Samson stops, looks into Ruth's eyes and says, 'I think you're a beautiful woman, Ruth.'

Ruth giggles. 'Wasn't that what you said to Eve earlier?'

Samson grins back. 'So she did tell you other women! I can't help it. I'm surrounded by lovely ladies. Do you not find me handsome?'

'You are a fine-looking man, Samson,' Ruth replies. 'No woman in her right mind would refuse you. If it were a different time and place, I would be delighted that you had called me beautiful, but we are here, in the Lord God's tent. He has brought us together for a reason. We must focus on what he wants us to do.'

'Just a little kiss, then,' begs Samson.

Ruth just laughs and continues with the weaving.

Suddenly, without any warning, Samson throws down the weaving stick and storms out of the tent. He charges towards the main gate in the wall. Ruth quickly calls to the others to wake up. Yawning and rubbing their eyes, they stumble out in search of Samson. When they reach him, they can't believe how much damage he has already done to the main wall. There is rubble everywhere. Despite his great strength and all the damage he's managed to cause, though, he cannot destroy the wall, and he can't move the gate at all.

Samson is stamping up and down and yelling, 'This blasted gate! The time I was in Gaza I pulled up their city gate, and it was twice the size of this one!' Even as he speaks, however, he seems to be calming down and giving up his escape attempt.

'Where were you hoping to go?' Rahab asks. 'We don't know

how we got here, so we certainly don't know what's on the other side of that gate.'

'I don't know where I was going,' Samson replies. 'I was just getting fed up with being here.'

'It's difficult for all of us,' says Saul quietly. 'I had a really hard time for the first day or two. Just don't fight it, Samson. It's the Lord God who has brought us here. Trust in him.'

'That's right!' Moses adds.

'I'm still totally fed up,' Samson shouts. 'I'm off to the Holy of Holies to have a word with the Lord God.' He storms back into the tent, enters the Holy of Holies and bellows, 'Lord God, listen to me now!'

'Tell me what's on your mind.' The voice of the Lord God is soothing. Samson takes a deep breath and grows slightly calmer. 'I'm fed up with being here. I want you to send me back to wherever you got me from.'

'What's caused this mood?' asks the Lord God.

'Women!' Samson roars. 'You created me a man. I like women. I am attracted to the women here. I would like to be with a woman. Why can't that be so?'

'Your track record with women is good!' the Lord God answers. 'Do I need to remind you about Delilah? She was your downfall, Samson. I would have thought that you could do with a break from women.'

'Yes, yes!' Samson retorts. 'That silly girl did betray me, but that was her. That was then. I want a woman now!'

'I think that's going to be pretty unlikely,' replies the Lord God.

'Then I want to get out of here!' Samson rushes out of the Holy of Holies. He charges towards a tree some distance away and flops down beneath it. The others decide to leave him there to quieten down.

Saul calls over to David, 'I believe it's our turn to do some weaving now.' They stroll over to the loom, where they have to ask Ruth to remind them how to do it. She jokes that, as men, they are as good as useless! Once Saul and David are able to demonstrate that they know what they were doing, Ruth heads off to bed.

David grins at Saul. 'Not in a million years did I ever expect to be sitting here with you, late at night, weaving at a loom!' They both laugh.

'You know, Saul,' he continues, 'I always thought that you were hard done by. I can tell you that now. There was that time when you were told by the Lord God to go and slaughter the Amalekites, and you spared Agag and some of the best sheep and cattle. I never felt you did anything too bad, and yet, because of that, the Lord God rejected you as king.'[44]

'I'm glad you think that,' Saul replies. 'I could never understand why the Lord God was so harsh with me. I mean, look at what you got up to with that Bathsheba woman—adultery, murder—and you still got forgiven! The Lord God always had it in for me.'

'Why did you disobey the Lord God that day?' David asks. 'He told you to slaughter all the Amalekites.'

'My men and I wanted to make sacrifices to God to thank him for the great victory.'

'I can understand that,' says David, 'but what the Lord God says goes.'

'I've come to realize that!' Saul says ruefully.

'I don't mean to bring this up.' David hesitates before going on. 'But I have to ask you about the priests of Nob. Why on earth did you kill 85 priests that day, and all the men, women, children and cattle?[45] It sounds like the work of a madman!'

'I can't even begin to give you an answer to that, David,' answers Saul. 'I spoke to you a day or two ago about my jealousy of you. It was an insane jealousy. After being rejected by the Lord God, and seeing your popularity and success, it truly drove me mad. I don't really wish to discuss any of that further.'

'Let's leave it, then,' David responds immediately. 'Let's focus on this ridiculous weaving instead!' They both laugh and continue chatting for the next couple of hours, having a good time, drinking a little wine. Who would have thought that these two could get on like this?

Eventually the time comes for them to finish and go to bed.

When they get to their sleeping area, they wake up Joseph and Moses, as it's their turn to weave. Moses wakes up quite grumpily. 'There should be a law against this!' Joseph tells him to forget about laws for once.

They make their way into the main living area and size up the loom. After a few initial difficulties, they manage to continue with the piece of cloth that the others have been working on.

'What did you think of Samson's behaviour earlier?' Moses asks.

'He's a strange man,' Joseph replies thoughtfully. 'He seems to love women too much. If he can't get what he wants, he sulks!'

'He's certainly not happy here,' Moses says decisively. 'I think I'll vote for him to leave tomorrow. It seems to be what he wants.'

'I was thinking the same,' is Joseph's response as he tries to untangle a knot in the yarn.

The two of them continue weaving for the next two hours, and when their time is up they wake up the next team—Joshua and Rahab. When these two get to the loom, they are surprised to see that the piece of cloth is now almost long enough to make a child's cloak.

'I can't believe that the men have been working on this for the last few hours! It actually looks quite good,' says Rahab.

'We're not all useless, Rahab.' Joshua flexes his muscular right arm. 'You know, I never really had time after the destruction of Jericho to thank you for the help you gave the Israelites. You saved the life of my spies, and you gave us the information we needed. Why did you do this for us?'

'It was just like I told your spies,' says Rahab. 'I knew that the Lord was going to give you the land. There were so many stories going around about what your God had done for you—the parting of the Red Sea, those plagues sent to punish the Egyptians. I have to admit that I was terrified about what might happen to us.[46]

'It wasn't just fear I felt, though. I had a real respect for the God of the Israelites. As you know, Joshua, I have a past I'm not proud of. I was a prostitute, and I was treated like dirt in my city. The talk of this great God of yours had a deep effect on me. I sensed that, at some stage in the future, this new God would mean something to me, even change my life.

'When your two spies visited me under the pretext of "wanting a little business", we got talking straight away. I knew they were from out of town. When I realized they were Israelites, I was so excited. We talked about your great God, and it was clear that he had led the spies to me. I immediately wanted to do everything I could do to help. They told me the city would soon be destroyed, and I begged them to spare my life and the lives of my family. It worked out in a remarkable way.'

'Yes, it did indeed,' says Joshua. 'You ended up being the great-great-whatever it was-grandmother of King David! Like I said earlier, I never did thank you properly for what you did. God bless you, Rahab.'

'Would you like some wine?' Rahab asks.

'No thank you. It's either too late or too early for a drink!' They laugh together. For the next couple of hours they chat away, and still manage to add a good length to the cloth.

At the end of their time, Joshua goes to the men's sleeping quarters and wakes up Noah, while Rahab wakes up Eve. They are the last pair for the weaving, and it is almost morning. By the time Eve and Noah finish their work, the others will be getting out of bed, thinking about breakfast.

Noah and Eve have obviously been sleeping deeply as they are very drowsy and don't say a great deal to one another as they weave. Even so, they exchange a few remarks about Samson's bizarre behaviour the night before.

DAY FIVE

As Noah and Eve reach the end of their weaving session, the others began to stir and come into the main living area. They are amazed and proud at the final length of the cloth, which would make a fine door-hanging for the tent. The only person missing is Samson, who is still outside somewhere.

The Lord God makes an announcement. 'Good morning. The task I set you last night has been completed successfully. Well done; it's an excellent piece of work. Before I explain what I would like you to do today, you should eat your morning meal, and then you must vote on the next member of the group to leave.'

Eve says that she will prepare some food for them all. Ruth offers to help. Joseph and Noah tell the others that they'll go outside and find Samson to let him know that it will soon be time to eat.

Not long after, Joseph and Noah rush back inside the tent, looking quite concerned. Joseph pants, 'He's nowhere to be seen!'

'Who?' asks Moses.

'Samson, of course!' gasps Noah. 'We've searched everywhere. We went to his favourite honey spot, checked under all the trees. We even peeked into the women's quarters to see if he had sneaked in there, but he has truly disappeared.'

David suggests that they should all split up and look for him.

Just as they are about to begin, they hear the Lord God. 'Samson has gone. When he ran out last night, he spent even more time trying to smash down the wall and rip up the gate. He was desperate, so I decided to open the gate. Without even hesitating, Samson ran through. Where he is now is my business. As far as the rest of you are concerned, he has left the tent. You must now eat your meal and prepare to vote for the next person who will leave.'

'It's certainly going to be a little quieter around the place with Samson gone,' says Saul.

'I was really getting to like the big man,' Joseph adds, with a shake of the head.

'Now there are only nine of us, and soon it will be down to eight.' Rahab looks a little worried.

'Let's just go along with the Lord God's wishes,' says Ruth firmly. 'We'll sit and eat now and prepare to vote.'

'Good idea,' Moses agrees. 'Let's follow the rules!'

'You and your rules!' laughs Saul.

After the light meal, the Lord God tells them to come and vote. David is asked to enter the Holy of Holies first. He does so, and immediately starts explaining that he would have voted for Samson to leave, had he still been around. Now he finds it difficult to choose. He eventually nominates Noah, but gives no real reason.

Saul nominates Moses, explaining that he's never heard anyone go on about rules so much! Ruth also nominates Noah, but she too has no real reason for doing so. Rahab immediately gives David's name again. She still can't seem to get the Bathsheba incident out of her head.

Joshua chooses Saul for the second time. He explains that even though Saul seems to have improved somewhat, there is still something he doesn't like about the man. Moses also picks on Saul, for much the same reason.

Unexpectedly, Joseph names Eve. Perhaps it's the 'bringing sin into the world' thing that bothers him. He makes no attempt to explain why he chose her. Noah also says, 'Eve', without giving any particular reason.

Finally, Eve nominates Noah, after a lot of puzzling and head-shaking. She explains that it's really difficult to choose someone to leave the tent.

When they have finished, the Lord God asks them to sit down in the main living area. There is a pause and then he announces: 'The person who will leave the tent today is…'—nobody speaks or even seems to breathe—'… Noah!'

Relieved and also saddened, the others surround Noah, some of them hugging him.

'It seems that you don't have much need for a boat builder then,' says Noah, and they manage to laugh.

'Noah, you have a few moments for your goodbyes,' says the Lord God. 'Then make your way towards the main gate.'

Everyone tells Noah that it was wonderful meeting him. They walk with him to the gate. After a few final hugs and pats on the back, the gate opens. Noah walks into the dazzling light beyond the gate, which closes behind him.

'I wonder what's out there,' says Saul, half to himself.

'We'll all find out sooner or later,' Moses replies. 'I don't know why, but I seem to have a vague memory of coming from a place that was beautiful and light. But I'm not sure if it's a memory or a dream.'

Some of the others are amazed at hearing him say this, because it turns out that they too have a vague sense of being taken from some beautiful place. They can remember their lives up to the point when they died. The next instant, they found themselves here in the Lord God's tent. As the conversation continues about what's beyond the gate, though, they each reveal that after they died they had found themselves in another place, but not one of them can explain it or remember anything about it clearly. Ruth concludes the discussion by saying, 'We can only trust the Lord God as we've always done. There will be a reason for all this.'

'Amen to that!' Moses declares.

When they have returned to the tent, Rahab asks, 'I wonder what the plan is now.'

No sooner has she said this than they all hear the Lord God's voice: 'I would like you to seat yourselves around the table, please.'

They follow the Lord God's instructions. When they're all ready in silence, the Lord God continues. 'I would now like to ask you all a question, sitting here at this table. You will answer, one at a time, in front of everyone. This is it: if you could have broken or made any law during your lives, what would it have been, and why? Eve will answer first.'

'This will be a good question for you, Moses,' smiles David. 'I don't think there are any other laws to make. I think you made them all!'

The others find this very funny. Even Moses manages a small grin. Then they fall silent, waiting for Eve's answer.

'I feel a bit awkward about this,' she begins. 'I only had one law to obey, and I couldn't even manage that. By breaking it, I spoilt everything for the rest of you.'

'Don't be silly,' says Ruth. 'We've talked about that already. Try to answer the Lord God's question.'

'Well,' Eve continues. 'I only had one law, and I broke it. So I suppose the only law I would have made would have been: "No laws must ever be made, so there will be no laws ever to break." I wish it had been like that in the beginning. It seems that as soon as we have laws and rules we can't help but break them.'

'That's a nice idea,' says Saul, 'but such a law would never have lasted, because someone like Moses would have come along and made lots of other rules.'

'Very funny!' responds Moses shortly. 'I believe it's your turn to answer now, Joseph.'

Joseph looks round at them all before saying, 'I think we need a law about how parents treat their children, and before you rush to tell me that there are plenty of laws concerning this, Moses, I'm referring to parents not having favourites.

'My brothers tried to kill me, they eventually sold me into slavery and, to cut a long story short, I ended up in prison. But, you know, I don't blame them in the slightest. My father Jacob loved me more than anything. He gave me a beautiful coat; I received all his attention. No wonder my brothers hated me and were jealous. I would have behaved in exactly the same way.

'My life turned out well in the end, and what happened was obviously part of the Lord God's plan to save his people from starvation, but I went through hell for years and it all started because I was my father's favourite. If I could have made a law, it would have ensured that parents never had favourites. It causes nothing but problems.'

'That sounds fair to me,' comments Rahab.

'Now we come to the Law Man himself,' laughs David. 'What other law would you have made or broken in your life?'

Moses says nothing for a while. Eventually he begins, 'You have made fun of me for days now, mocking me and the laws that I made. Do you think that I wanted to make them? It was the Lord God who made those laws. He just transmitted them through me. And it was his chosen people who needed those laws. I got so fed up with their moaning and complaining. The Lord God performed great miracles for his people, leading them out of Egypt, providing food and water, yet still they turned away from him. They needed laws to teach them what was right and wrong. Believe it or not, I hated the fact that all those laws were required.

'Don't jeer at me as if I loved rules and laws. I hate them! I certainly would not have wanted to make any others!'

The others are taken back by Moses' vehemence. He continues, 'I hope that one day the Lord God will send someone who can get rid of all the laws, maybe just reduce them to one or two, such as 'Love the Lord God with all your heart and love each other.' If we truly followed this law, I'm sure we'd obey the rest of the old laws as well.'

'Why didn't you just say this years ago instead of presenting people with all the laws?' David asks.

'Back then, that one law wouldn't have been enough for the people,' replies Moses. 'Many of them had little respect or love for the Lord God.'

'That makes sense,' says Ruth. 'Thank you for sharing that, Moses. Now it's your turn, Joshua. What law would you have broken or made if you had had the chance?'

'I don't want to upset the Lord God,' Joshua answers promptly, 'but I have to say that I really did want to disobey him on many occasions. It was so hard serving him sometimes, when the people did nothing but complain.'

'I know how you must have felt,' says Moses grimly.

Joshua continues, 'The time the Lord God commanded me to march around the walls of Jericho for seven days caused me nothing but trouble. Many of the people thought I had gone mad and couldn't understand why we were marching in silence once a day for six days. Even I started to question what I was doing. I felt like disobeying everything. I think that if I could have made a law back then, it would have been to cut out anyone's tongue who continually complained about me and God's commands.'

'That sounds a little harsh,' Eve frowns.

'Nothing harsh about it!' says Moses. 'It's quite understandable.'

'Yes, it does sound harsh,' Joshua admits. 'I wouldn't really have gone ahead with it, but I certainly felt like doing so at times!'

The others then ask Rahab to give her answer to the Lord God's question.

Rahab speaks quietly. 'If I could have made a rule, it would have been that no one should ever look down on prostitutes or treat them like dirt. Not one woman I knew who was a prostitute chose to be so. We women were treated like dirt generally. I desperately needed money to support my parents and myself, and disgusting men were prepared to pay good money to sleep with me. It's a terrible, terrible thing that any woman at any time should be reduced to making money this way. I'm so glad that I found the Lord God and that he changed my whole life. That's all any of these women ever want, to be taken away from their horrible way of life. I hope that prostitutes everywhere will be able to know God's love, and have him change their lives, give their lives meaning.'

'That was lovely to hear, Rahab,' says Ruth, and she gives Rahab a warm hug. Rahab then asks Ruth for her answer to the question.

'There is no law that I would ever break,' Ruth says carefully, 'and there is no law that I would ever want to make. I wish for nothing else than to serve the Lord God.'

'Is that it?' asks Saul. 'I was hoping for something a little more exciting than that!'

'Well, come on, Saul,' David nudges him. 'What's your answer?'

'I wish,' says Saul, 'that I had made a law stating that if any of my commanders ever thought I was going a little mad, or turning insanely jealous, they should immediately relieve me of command and, if necessary, put me to death. That would have saved me and poor David here from a great deal of misery.'

'I think that sounds as if it would have been a great law!' David bursts out laughing and the others join in.

'What about you, David?' Saul asks.

'I wish I had made a law that would have forbidden me from ever doing what I did with Bathsheba and Uriah, her husband. King or no king, I should have been put to death immediately. I know people have been very shocked by this event in my life and I don't blame them. I deserved to have died for doing such a terrible thing.'

'It's all been talked over now, David,' says Moses. 'It's quite clear to us how much you regret what happened. We don't need to discuss it any more.' The others agree.

'Thank you for answering that question,' the Lord God announces. 'You may now have the next few hours free. After that I will call you back to the table.'

By now, everyone in the group just wants to rest, or lie down, as they have all been up at some stage during the previous night for the weaving. The women go back to their sleeping quarters. Saul and David decide to relax in the pool outside for a while, and the other men disappear for a rest.

It seems as if only a few moments have passed when they hear the Lord God calling them back to the table. Once they are gathered, he says, 'Over the last five days, you have been able to eat what you want and drink as much wine as you want. From now on, that will change. You may drink as much water as you wish, but no more food will be provided.'

David nips outside to see if the animals are still there, or the ingredients for baking bread. There is nothing left. The Lord God has removed it all. He runs back and tells the others the bad news.

'Are we going to starve to death?' Joseph demands of the Lord God.

'Don't worry,' Moses breaks in. 'In the wilderness the people continually worried about starving, but the Lord provided. Let's see what else the Lord God has to say.'

The Lord God continues, 'There will be some food to eat, but only if you fulfil the next tasks. I will set you riddles to solve or practical challenges to perform. If you are successful, you will receive enough food for one meal. Your first task, though, is to go and hunt for some food. I will allow you to walk through the main gates soon. Instead of a bright light, you will find a wilderness beyond. You will have a few hours to hunt for food, which you may eat this evening, when I will also provide you with some wine. If you fail to catch anything, you will go to bed with nothing but water in your stomachs. Outside the tent, you will find some items that may help you!'

The men are immediately excited at the prospect of hunting. Moses tells them about being brought up as a prince in Egypt and all the hunting techniques he learned. The other men also share their experiences. For once they are relishing the task before them. After the initial excitement and sharing of stories, they walk outside to see what the Lord God has given them. There is a selection of bows and arrows, spears, knives, nets and tools for digging pits.

Moses says to the others, 'Bearing in mind that we only have a few hours for hunting, I don't think we will have time to dig pits as traps. I think we should take the bows, arrows and spears.'

They all agree with his suggestion. The men arm themselves with a bow each and a selection of arrows, a spear and a knife. The women volunteer to take a few nets, in case they are needed to trap wounded animals. With no time to spare, they quickly drink some water from the well and the women fill up a few skinfuls to take with them. Then they head towards the gates, which have swung open.

As they walk through, they see a vast grassy plain ahead of them. There are plenty of trees around, and bushy areas where animals might graze. It is ideal hunting terrain. The men know this, and grow even more excited at the prospect of the hunt.

'There could be plenty of wild animals out here—possibly lions,' David remarks. 'We'll need to be very careful.'

Saul adds that, if they are lucky, they may find a herd of deer. The thought of venison makes their mouths water. A short distance ahead of them is a small hill, and Joshua suggests that it would make a good vantage point to look out for game, so they cautiously make their way up the slope.

Once at the top, they have a great view over the plains below, and it isn't long before they spot plenty of game scattered around.

'The Lord provides!' Moses says in a loud whisper.

'Yes, but we have to catch them!' Eve responds in a normal voice, and the men tell her to speak more quietly.

'Have faith, Eve,' says David. 'Today is a good day to hunt.' After further discussion, they settle on a plan of action. On the other side of the hill is a dense patch of trees. The plan is to use this screen to help them sneak as close as possible to the animals before launching any weapons. The wind is also blowing in the right direction, so there is no chance of their scent being picked up. After some careful stalking, they end up no more than a spear's throw from a large group of deer.

You can see the smiles on some of the men's faces; they're loving this. They may be only moments away from a very successful hunt.

Suddenly, the deer in front of them scarper. Within seconds, every one of them has disappeared.

'What happened there?' asks David.

'Not one of us made a sound, and we were downwind of them.' Saul straightens up, looking discouraged.

David's face changes. Clearly he understands what has just happened. 'I think we've got company,' he says.

'What do you mean?' asks Ruth.

'Well, for years I was a shepherd, and not a day went by when I didn't have to scare off wild animals. The sheep would suddenly scatter just as that herd of game did there. It means only one thing. There are lions nearby.'

'You're joking!' says Rahab anxiously.

'Don't panic,' Saul replies. 'I notice that David has his sling with him. It's the lions that should be scared, not us. I've told you before how David killed the giant Goliath with nothing more than his sling.'

'And my faith in the Lord!' David adds, pulling the sling from his belt. He is about to continue when Eve suddenly screams. To her right, far too close for comfort, two lionesses are heading straight towards them.

'Get down. Stay totally still and silent,' David shouts to the others. 'Moses, I want you to take your bow and aim at the animal on the right. I'll use my sling to hit the one on the left.'

Moses nods in agreement. Scenting danger, the lionesses start to charge towards them. David is already swinging his sling around his head and takes aim. It's a perfect shot! The lioness growls ferociously, but stops in her tracks and then bounds off. Moses' arrow is also aimed perfectly. It strikes the other animal, not piercing the skin deeply but doing enough to shock her and send her running. When the lionesses are safely gone, the hunters breathe a collective sigh of relief and congratulate David and Moses.

Almost with the same breath, David and Moses say how fighting off wild animals brings back fond memories of their own hunting days.

While they are both reminiscing, Saul and Joshua have drawn arrows and are walking quietly towards a cluster of trees in front of them. Just beyond is a solitary deer, fairly young, but large enough to provide enough meat for them all that evening. The others stay back a little, so as not to disturb the hunt. The women quietly get the nets ready in case they are needed to trap the animal.

Saul and Joshua move on tiptoe, checking the ground before taking a step so as not to make the slightest noise and risk startling the animal. Eventually they nod to one another, signalling that they are now within striking distance.

As quietly as they can, they draw their bows and take aim. They are both well-built men, and there is a fair bit of power behind those poised arrows.

They release their arrows simultaneously. Two excellent shots hit the animal in the neck, stunning but not killing it. David and Moses both sprint towards it, each with a spear. Joseph and the women are close behind, bringing the nets. When David and Moses are close enough, they throw their spears. Once again, both men have aimed perfectly, and hit the deer in the chest. It falls to the ground but still struggles violently. The others throw the net over the animal to prevent it from escaping.

Moses takes a knife, utters a prayer of thanks to the Lord God for a successful hunt, and slits the deer's throat. In the middle of all the excitement, David reminds them that other predators will soon pick up the scent of fresh blood, so they must hurry and keep the celebratory noise down until they are at their tent, within the safety of the walls.

David, Moses and Saul help to carry the carcass back. Joshua and the others keep an eye out for any wild animals that might be lurking around.

They eventually reach the wall and, as they walk through the gates, they mysteriously close behind them. It is then that they let out a huge cheer and break into a celebratory dance, praising God for a successful hunt and for keeping them safe.

Just then they hear the Lord God's voice: 'I congratulate you on a successful hunt. Your challenge was to find your own food, and you have succeeded. As a reward you will have wine to drink and all the ingredients you need to prepare a feast. Before you begin, however, it is time for you to vote out another person from the tent, and we will begin right now. David, please report to the Holy of Holies.'

One minute they were all celebrating, the next minute there is silence.

'At least we should have been able to eat first,' growls Saul.

'It is a little unfair,' adds Joseph.

'But who are we to complain or question the Lord God?' asks Ruth.

'Ruth's right,' says Rahab. 'Let's just follow his command and get it over and done with.'

David heads for the Holy of Holies. Once inside, the Lord God asks him to nominate somebody. 'I nominate Joseph,' David says, 'for no other reason than that he didn't really take part in the hunt.'

Then it is Saul's turn, and he gives the same answer. He feels that Joseph should have been far more involved in the hunt. He even describes Joseph as a bit of a 'mummy's boy'!

Ruth also nominates Joseph, but her reason is that he has seemed a little quiet of late, even a bit dreamy! She has decided to choose him to go, as this might be what Joseph actually wants.

Rahab nominates Moses, but doesn't give any special reason.

Joshua and Moses also vote for Joseph, giving the same reason as the other men. None of them is overly impressed with his hunting skills!

Joseph then makes his way into the Holy of Holies and says to the Lord God, 'I would like to thank you for the dream that you gave me last night, letting me know that I would be evicted this evening. In my dream I could see an animal running from me, and yet I made no effort to catch it. Then I saw myself walking into the light through the gate. When I woke up this morning, the meaning of the dream was clear. I knew I would be leaving soon. I really don't know who to vote for, but if I must say something, knowing already that it is me leaving soon, I choose Saul.'

Eve nominates Moses. She finds him too intense!

The Lord God summons them to the main living area of the tent. He tells them that it is time for the fourth leave-taking. As they are sitting there, and before the Lord God can speak again, Joseph stands up. 'I know my hunting skills weren't up to much, and I know the men here weren't impressed with that, and quite rightly you voted for me to go.'

'Were you spying on us in the Holy of Holies?' asks David.

'Not at all,' replies Joseph. 'Last night I had a dream that I would leave today. I knew that we would be going on a hunt, and I knew that I wouldn't be much use. And I saw myself walking through the gate.'

'That's amazing!' says Moses. 'I voted for you to be evicted for exactly that reason. It was nothing personal. I had to vote, and as we had just come back from the hunt, that was the first excuse I could think of for choosing somebody to go.'

'None of you has to explain,' Joseph smiles. 'It has been a wonderful experience, and I will miss you all, yet I suspect we will see each other again very soon.'

'I also sense that,' says Ruth quietly.

They all embrace Joseph and slowly make their way to the gate, talking together as they go. When they get there, Joseph turns to them and says, 'I will see you again very soon.' As it has done before, the gate opens and the beautiful light begins to shine through. Joseph gives his friends a final wave and walks into the light. The gates close slowly behind him.

Before any of them has time to feel sad, Joshua calls out, 'Let's get back and prepare our feast!' Filled with fresh enthusiasm, they hurry back to the tent.

Over the next few hours, the seven of them work together preparing the meal. The men skin the deer and prepare the meat for cooking. The women collect herbs and vegetables, and when the meat is ready they put all the ingredients into a huge pot and start cooking a stew.

Before long, the aroma of the food wafts around. They are all starving and can't wait to begin this magnificent meal. When it is nearly ready, Ruth suggests that they sit around the table and ask David to teach them a song.

When they are gathered, David says, 'Here is a song I once wrote, praising the Lord God as the supreme ruler.'

'That sounds good,' says Saul.

'Yes! Let's praise the Lord God,' calls out Moses.

David sings the following song three times through.

Let's clap our hands for joy, everybody!
Let's praise the Lord God with loud songs!
The Lord God our King is to be feared;
He is a wonderful King, and he rules the whole world.

He gave us victory over the people;
And he made us rule the nations.
He chose the land in which we were to live,
The proud and wonderful possession of his people,
Whom he loves.

The Lord God goes up to his throne.
There are great shouts of joy and huge blasts of trumpets,
as the Lord God goes up.
Sing praise to the Lord God;
Sing praise to our king!
The Lord God is king over all the world;
Let's praise him with great songs.

The Lord God sits on his sacred throne;
He rules over the nations.
The rulers of the nations all gather together
With the people of the God of Abraham.
He is more powerful than all the armies;
The Lord God is our supreme ruler.[47]

David teaches them the words and the simple melody. They sing enthusiastically, making a truly joyful noise to the Lord.

When the singing is over, the food is finally ready. The women serve the food; the men pour the wine. When they are gathered at the table, Eve utters the words of thanksgiving.

When they have finally finished eating and are sitting round drinking wine, the Lord God makes another announcement.

'For the rest of this evening, you may simply enjoy being with one another, and drink the wine that I have provided! Tomorrow I will be asking each of you five questions to show how much you actually know about each other, as you have been together for nearly six days now.'

Joshua sings out, 'Well, that sounds easy enough!' and sits looking smug.

The Lord God continues, 'The two of you who get most questions correct tomorrow will be allowed to stay, and may eat and drink plenty. The other five will all have to leave.'

Joshua doesn't look so smug now!

'Let's not spoil our evening now,' says Saul. 'Let's carry on enjoying ourselves, but let's make sure we tell each other lots of things about ourselves. As the Lord God said, we've been together for nearly six days, and we have learned so much about each other. We should have no problems tomorrow.'

'Whatever happens,' Ruth adds, 'it has been a wonderful time here, getting to know you all.'

'My great-grandma is right!' David laughs. 'Whatever happens happens.' The others agree.

Ruth pretends to frown at David. 'I do wish you would stop calling me great-grandma. It makes me feel so old!' There is laughter round the table.

They continue talking and enjoying the wine for the rest of the evening. They share stories about themselves, both good and bad. Eventually, the energetic time of hunting begins to take its toll. It is late. They are tired. It is time to sleep.

DAY SIX

It is still quite early when the Lord God's voice suddenly booms, 'Wake up!' Only two words, but the whole tent shakes! Within a few minutes, everyone is up. Some of the men seem to have aching heads. Everyone heads towards the washing area, but Joshua and David just jump straight into the pool outside. That certainly wakes them up, and apparently sorts out their headaches!

The Lord God himself has prepared a morning meal for them. The table is filled with fruit and bread, milk and honey. They all sit and eat. Joshua remarks, 'I'm not particularly hungry, but I suppose I'd better eat in case I'm one of the five thrown out. We might have to go on a long journey!'

The others nod in agreement and carry on eating hungrily.

A moment later, the Lord God tells them that when they have finished, they are to gather in the main living area of the tent and sit in a circle. Once the meal is over, and they are all in position, waiting quietly, the Lord God announces, 'I will now ask each of you five questions, one at a time. I will be testing how much you know about each other. I will even question you about those who have already left—Noah, Joseph, Deborah and Samson. I'm sure none of you will forget Samson!'

They laugh at this. The Lord God is right. How can anyone forget that big man?

'Moses,' says the Lord God. 'I will start with you. Your question is, "What was the size of the ark that Noah built?"'

'What an unfair question!' Moses grumbles. 'I remember Noah mentioning it at some stage, but I really have no idea. I know it was huge. Will that do?'

The others find this amusing. Eventually the Lord God says, 'Yes, Moses, it was huge, but to be more exact, the answer I was looking for was "300 cubits long, 50 cubits wide and 30 cubits high".[48] It was quite an outrageous size. People thought Noah was mad, building this massive ark in the middle of dry land. But his faith was strong. He built the ark, and you know the rest of the story. Moses, I'm afraid you answered incorrectly.

'The next question is for Joshua. This is not so much a factual question, but more to see what your personal response is. I will judge whether it is an acceptable answer. I want to see whether you really did listen to Ruth, so tell me what struck you most about her story.'

Joshua thinks deeply for a while. He then smiles over at Ruth, and says, 'What I remembered most was her loyalty to her mother-in-law, and her faith in God, which was amazing. I remember the words she said to Naomi. "Wherever you go, I will go... and your God will be my God." It's amazing that, even as a non-Jew, she received God's blessing. God's love can never be confined to one nation or one particular people group.'

When Joshua has finished, the others praise him for a wonderful answer. Ruth smiles back at him, and thanks him for having listened to her and understood. The Lord God tells Joshua that he has answered well.

Saul says to Joshua, 'It looks like you're on the way to eating well today.'

'It's only the first question,' replies Joshua.

'That's true,' says Moses, trying to make himself feel a little better, seeing as he answered incorrectly.

The Lord God continues. 'Now for your question, Eve. I'm sure you haven't forgotten our big friend Samson. Having listened to the story of his life, what would you say led to his downfall?'

Eve replies, 'Well, you probably all think it was my fault because I brought sin and evil into the world!'

The others realize that she is actually joking, but still feel they should remind her that they don't think that for one minute.

Smiling, Eve continues, 'From what I remember of the story, it was Samson trusting that deceitful woman Delilah that led to his final downfall. But I also remember him telling us that he was dedicated to God as a Nazarite, and as such he was not allowed to drink alcohol, go near a dead body or cut his hair. I believe that it was breaking all these promises that led to his downfall.'

'A perfect answer,' responds the Lord God. 'And now for you, Rahab. If you were to sum up the whole story of Joseph in just 20 words, how would you do it?'

'Now that's a tricky one!' exclaims Rahab. 'Give me a minute or two to work it all out.'

The others realize that this is indeed a difficult question. They wonder what she will say. Eventually she says with a cheeky grin, 'Here we go. "Jacob loved, brothers hated, slave Potiphar's, wife fancied, prison dreams, king's dreams, governor Egypt, test brothers, all united, Hebrews saved".'

'Brilliant!' they all shout. The Lord God says that Rahab has given a most excellent answer.

The Lord God then tells Saul to prepare for his question. 'Apart from the flood in Noah's story, Saul, who else in the tent mentioned something about a flood in their story? Briefly explain what happened.'

You can tell immediately that Saul is not happy with this question. His first response is, 'I think I'll be joining you on the water diet today, Moses.'

He thinks deeply for a moment, and then says, 'The story must have been told in the first day or two, when I was walking around sulking and not paying any attention. The only answer I can give is that I'm sure I heard Deborah saying something about a flood, but that's all that springs to mind.'

'If only you had paid a little more attention!' The Lord God replies. 'You are right to say "Deborah", but I need a bit more than that. Can anyone help Saul out?'

Ruth fills in the detail. 'The people of Israel were suffering under the violent rule of King Jabin, an invader from the north. It was

Deborah who roused the nation to action. At her command a military leader called Barak gathered 10,000 men to fight the evil King Jabin.

'Jabin's commander Sisera amassed his 900 chariots and men to meet the army of Israel. Barak attacked, and it was then that there was a flash flood. This flood swamped Sisera's chariots. It was a great victory for Israel.[49] I think this may have been the answer you were looking for, Lord God.'

'Indeed it was,' says the Lord God. 'Your turn, Ruth. Can you tell me what it was that first led to Saul being rejected as king?'

'Charming,' says Saul. 'Why do we have to drag all this up again?'

'There are lot of things we don't like hearing about our past,' David claps Saul on the shoulder. 'It's just a simple question. Let's see if Ruth can answer.'

Ruth says that she does remember David talking about it a few days ago. 'It was something to do with the Amalekites. I remember now! Samuel told Saul that the Lord God wanted to punish the people of Amalek because they had opposed the Israelites when they were coming out of Egypt. Saul was told to destroy everything they had—women, children and babies, the cattle, sheep...'

'Yes, yes,' says Saul gloomily. 'We remember.'

Ruth continues. 'Well, the fact is, Saul did defeat the Amalekites, but he captured King Agag of Amalek alive, and he didn't kill the best sheep and cattle, calves and lambs, or anything else that was good. It was because of this that the Lord God rejected him as king.'

'And to this day I've never understood that!' Saul says angrily. 'We only kept the best plunder to offer as a sacrifice to the Lord God.'

'Ah yes,' David replies. 'But which does the Lord God prefer—obedience or offerings and sacrifices?'

'Please,' says Saul, 'let's not go over all that again.'

The Lord God speaks: 'Ruth, your answer is correct. Finally, David, here is your first question. I'm sure you remember the story of when I first revealed myself to Moses. As you have a wonderful voice and a gift with words, I want you to compose a short song describing this story. I will tell you when to stop!'

Saul leans towards David. 'I'm glad it's you singing and not me.' David smiles. After a moment, he begins.

> *While looking after his sheep and goats,*
> *He came to Sinai;*
> *And then he saw a burning bush,*
> *Beneath the desert sky.*
>
> *The flames were bright and burning red,*
> *But something made him scratch his head;*
> *He thought that with a fire like this,*
> *That bush should surely now be dead.*
>
> *A voice then called to him by name… 'Moses!'*
> *He said 'I'm here, so what's your business?'*
> *'You'll remove your shoes and—'*

David starts to falter.

'That will do, David,' says the Lord God. 'Well done.' The others burst into applause.

At this point, the Lord God tells them that, after the first question, Moses and Saul are in last place, and face being asked to leave the tent. He tells them that it is time for the second question.

'I will now give you each a clay tablet and a sharp wedge that you can use for marking it. The answer to the next question will be a number. Each one of you will carve the number into your clay tablet. When I ask you, you will hold up your answer.

'The question is about our huge friend Samson who recently left you. During one evening when you were all eating and enjoying your wine, Samson told you about when he caught a lot of foxes and tied their tails together, two by two, and set fire to them. He then set them loose in the Philistine cornfields and destroyed their entire crop.[50] What I want to know is: how many foxes did Samson catch?'

'What sort of question is that?' asks David.

'I don't even think Samson told us the exact number, did he?' says Saul, who looks very worried at the prospect of not answering the second question correctly.

'He did,' Ruth replies. 'Maybe you both had too much wine that evening, and have forgotten what he told us.'

'I think she's right,' says Joshua with a sigh.

'You have a moment to think about this and carve your answer,' announces the Lord God.

They all start thinking, and eventually begin carving. Some are fairly confident, others are clearly guessing!

When the time is up, the Lord God gives the order to hold up their clay tablets.

Moses has written 500.

Joshua has written 1000.

Eve has written 300.

Rahab has written 300.

Saul has written 300.

Ruth has written 300.

David has written 100.

The Lord God gives the verdict: 'Samson told you that he caught 300 foxes. That's the right answer.'

David turns on Saul. 'You sneaky man! You claimed that Samson didn't even tell us the number. You knew all along!'

'Sorry, David,' replies Saul. 'But it does feel good to get one up on you!'

The others laugh at this, and even David sees the funny side.

After two questions, Moses is now clearly behind the others. Joshua, Saul and David have given one incorrect answer. Eve, Rahab and Ruth are in the lead.

'It would seem at the moment that women pay more attention!' Joshua remarks.

'I think we do,' says Rahab.

'Well, I'm not giving up yet,' Moses mutters. 'We still have three questions left.'

'Let us continue,' says the Lord God. 'Now to question three.

This one is for you, Moses, and I don't need to remind you that you need to get this one right.'

'Yes, yes,' says Moses. 'I don't need reminding.'

'Why did playing the harp become quite dangerous for David when he was around Saul? What incident am I talking about?'

'I think I might know this one,' Moses answers. 'I remember David telling me. It was when Saul was insanely jealous of him.'

'Less of the "insane", if you don't mind,' interrupts Saul.

'It was after David had killed Goliath,' Moses continues. 'During the celebrations the women sang, "Saul has killed thousands, but David tens of thousands!" This made Saul very jealous. The following day, he was in a foul mood, ranting and raving like a mad man.'

'Do we really need so much detail?' asks Saul.

'I'm just setting the scene,' Moses replies smoothly.

'Anyway, Saul wasn't too happy and, as usual, David went to play the harp to calm him. While he was playing, Saul threw a spear at him twice, and each time David had to dodge to save his own life. So, in answer to your question, Lord God, that is why it became dangerous for David to play the harp when he was around Saul.'

'A perfect answer,' says the Lord God.

They all cheer, including Moses, who is delighted to have got his first correct answer.

'Joshua,' says the Lord God. 'Now it is time for your third question.' They all quieten down and eagerly wait to hear what it is.

'Your question,' the Lord God goes on, 'is about our dear friend Joseph. It was thanks to Joseph being able to interpret the Pharaoh's dream that the Hebrews were saved. Can you tell me what this dream was and what it meant?'

You can tell straight away that Joshua isn't happy about this question.

'I know it was something to do with a famine,' he says slowly. 'Let me try to work it out. I'm sure it was about some fat sheep, or cows or something. That's it! It was cows!'

The others chuckle as they listen to Joshua stumbling through his answer.

'If you could finish sometime today…' says the Lord God, as he hesitates.

'I think I have it now,' Joshua exclaims, his face full of relief. 'There were some fat cows that came out of the river—obviously the Nile, as Joseph was in Egypt. Some thin cows also came out of the river, and they ate all the fat cows. After they had eaten, they were still as thin as before. From what I remember Joseph saying, the dream meant that there was going to be a bumper harvest for a good few years, and then an equal number of years of famine. I think it was six or seven years of each.

'The Pharaoh was troubled by this and didn't know what to do. Joseph came up with a cunning plan. The Pharaoh loved it, and made Joseph the governor of Egypt. How's that for an answer?'

'I'll accept it,' says the Lord God. 'It was actually seven fat and seven thin cows.'

'That's what I meant to say,' Joshua says, grinning.

The others applaud Joshua. That's two correct answers and only one wrong for him!

Now it's Eve's turn for a question, and so far she has answered two correctly. The Lord God says, 'Eve, you have heard Moses continually mentioning the Law over the days you have been together. I would like you to repeat for us the Ten Commandments that I gave Moses on Mount Sinai.[51] But this is how I want you to do it! I want you to mime each one of the commandments in order. Moses has told you all often enough what the commandments are, so you should be able to do this. When Moses thinks he is sure what it is that you are doing, he will ask you to explain the mime.'

'That's a tough one!' says David.

'You can do it, Eve,' shouts Rahab supportively.

So far Eve has two questions correct. Can she manage a third? She has quite a daunting task ahead of her.

She walks into the middle of the group and begins by pointing upwards with one finger. As she is looking upwards, she bows down. Moses asks her to explain herself.

'Worship no God but the Lord God,' Eve explains.

'That's one,' says Moses. 'Continue.'

Eve pretends that she is moulding something together with her hands. When she finishes, she puts the object on the floor and begins bowing down to it. After a while she stands up and gestures with her finger that it was wrong to do this.

Moses asks her to explain.

'The second commandment,' Eve answers, 'is that you are not to make any idols and worship them.'

'Well done,' says Moses. 'That's the first two done.'

The Lord God then interrupts, 'Well done, Eve. You have done enough. I would now like Rahab to continue with the next two commandments.'

Eve looks very relieved, but the others exchange worried glances. Perhaps they will all have to participate in this miming round.

Rahab takes her place in the middle and starts by pointing upwards. She forms the Lord God's name with her lips and then laughs. She continues mouthing 'the Lord God' and laughing. She also gestures with her hands that the name 'God' means nothing. Moses nods his head and asks her to explain what she has done.

'I was saying the Lord God's name and then laughing at it,' Rahab says. 'The third commandment makes it very clear that we must not take God's name in vain.'

'Perfectly put,' says Moses.

Rahab starts miming the fourth commandment. First, she gestures with her finger the number 1. When she has done this, she lies down on the floor and pretends to sleep. She then gets up and makes bowing movements as if worshipping the Lord God. At this point, Moses guesses that Rahab is correct, so he asks her to explain the mime.

'The fourth commandment is that we must keep one day a week for rest and worship,' she replies.

'Exactly!' says Moses.

The Lord God announces that it is now Saul's turn.

Saul stands in the middle and pretends to hold a knife or weapon of some sort. He mimes walking up to someone and attacking them, making it quite clear that he has killed them. Next he waves his finger, indicating that he shouldn't have done that.

Moses stops the mime and asks Saul to explain himself.

'The fifth commandment is that we should not murder.'

'Oh dear,' says Moses. 'The commandment against murder is number six. Commandment number five is that we must respect our parents.'

'Moses is correct,' the Lord God decrees. 'I'm afraid that Saul scores no points in this round. I would now like David to take his turn.'

As David gets up, he starts protesting. 'Why must I do this next mime? I'm fed up with being reminded of my past and the incident with Bathsheba. Is this some kind of wicked joke?'

One or two of the others can't help smirking.

'Right,' says Moses. 'Just tell us what the seventh commandment is, and we'll let you have the point.'

'Do not commit adultery,' David snaps, arms folded. 'There, are you all satisfied now?'

'Not as satisfied as Bathsheba was,' Saul jokes.

David gives Saul a filthy look and sits down.

Ruth realizes that it's now her turn. She starts off by glancing around suspiciously, and then pretends to take something and run off. Moses seems convinced and asks her to explain.

'Commandment number eight is, "Do not steal".'

'Yes, it is,' says Moses, 'and what about number nine?'

Ruth has to think about this one. It appears that she knows the commandment, but finds it difficult to mime. At last she has an idea. She lies down on the floor, then stands up again, and gestures with her finger that she shouldn't have done that. Moses laughs at this, realizing that it was quite a clever mime, and he asks her to explain.

Ruth says confidently, 'Do not lie!'

'Very clever,' Joshua says, and leads the others in a round of applause.

The Lord God asks Moses to mime the last commandment. He

does so by looking at each member of the group, gesturing with his hands and face to show that he really longs for something that they each possess. He twists his face into a mask of desperation to show how badly he wants it.

The Lord God asks him to explain himself, and Moses tells them all that the final commandment is not to be jealous of what someone else has got. Although the others applaud his effort, he doesn't get a point for this, as he was the one who received the Ten Commandments. He would have looked rather stupid if he didn't get them right!

After three questions, Eve, Rahab and Ruth are in the lead, having answered all their questions correctly.

Joshua and David are in second place.

Saul and Moses are in last place, and could soon be thrown out.

The Lord God announces that to finish this game, he will ask them two final questions, beginning with David. They all quieten down and wait for him to begin.

'David,' the voice of the Lord God booms. 'I have two questions to ask you about Eve. First, what fruit was it that she ate and then gave to Adam? Second, when Eve and Adam realized that they were both naked, what did they use to cover themselves?'

Already David looks a little confused. He starts to think aloud. 'Now then, was it an apple? Let me see. I don't think Eve ever told us what the fruit was. I think she simply said that the fruit came from the tree that gave knowledge of what is good and what is bad.' He nods to himself and then announces, 'The forbidden fruit came from the tree that gave knowledge of what is good and what is bad. The answer to the second question is that Eve and Adam sewed fig leaves together to cover themselves.'

'Well done, David,' says the Lord God. 'That's two correct for you. You have answered four out of five questions correctly. You're still in with a chance of staying one more night. Ruth, it is time for your last two questions. I would like to ask you about Saul. First, when Saul went to visit the witch of Endor, whose spirit did he want to contact?'

'How embarrassing!' interrupts Saul. The others tell him to keep quiet.

'My second question,' continues the Lord God, 'is on which mountain did Saul commit suicide?'

'Well, why don't you just rub it in?' Saul grumbles.

'Be quiet, Saul,' says David. 'We're all having bits of our past dragged up from time to time. You're being treated no different from the rest of us.'

Ruth answers confidently, 'It was the spirit of Samuel that Saul summoned, and it was on Mount Gilboa that he killed himself.'[52]

'Excellent!' exclaims the Lord God. 'You have answered all five questions correctly. Now, Saul, it's your two questions.'

'Make them easy, will you please, dear Lord?' Saul begs. The others laugh.

The Lord God continues, 'For you, Saul, I have two questions about David.'

'My, my. The Lord God really does have a sense of humour,' Saul mutters half under his breath.

'My first question is this,' the Lord God goes on, ignoring Saul's comment. 'When Bathsheba gave birth to her second son, I ordered Nathan to name the boy Jedidiah. What name did David give to the boy?'

'That's an easy one,' Saul replies. 'It was Solomon.'[53]

'Well done,' says the Lord God. 'My second question is this…' Saul looks fairly confident now, having managed the first question. What about the next one? 'At what stage in the story of David did I once say this: "Man looks at the outward appearance, but I look at the heart"?'

'How on earth am I supposed to know that?' asks Saul, sounding rather fed up. 'I have no idea!'

The Lord God asks whether anybody else might know the answer. Ruth waves a hand tentatively. 'I think this is the story David told us about when Samuel went to Bethlehem looking for the next king. At first he saw some of David's other brothers, who were tall and good-looking, like Eliab and Abinadab, and because of the way they looked he presumed that it might be one of them. It was at this point that the Lord God said, "Pay no attention to how tall and handsome he is. I have rejected him, because I do not judge as man judges. Man looks at the outward appearance, but I look at the heart."'[54]

David tells Ruth that she has told the story perfectly.

The Lord God says to Saul, 'Overall, you have only answered two questions correctly. You may well be leaving soon.'

Saul subsides huffily as the Lord God says to Rahab, 'It's now over to you, and so far you have answered all your questions correctly. Rahab, I have two questions about Samson. Could you tell me the name of his father, and could you tell me the name of the Philistine god whose temple Samson destroyed when he also died?'

Rahab answers immediately: 'I know that the Philistine god was Dagon, but I can't remember the name of Samson's father. Something tells me his name started with the letter "M", but I am really not sure.'

'Well, Rahab, you got the name of that heathen god correct,' says the Lord God. 'It was indeed Dagon. Samson's father was called Manoah. That means you got four out of five questions correct, which is a good score.' The others congratulate her.

'And now, Eve, here are your two last questions. You've spent a lot of time chatting to Ruth, so your questions will be about her. First, when Naomi, Ruth's mother-in-law, returned to Bethlehem, the women of the town were excited and asked, "Is this really Naomi?" Naomi did not wish to be known by her name, which meant "pleasant". What name did she choose instead?'

'Only yesterday Ruth and I were talking about this!' Eve says excitedly. 'Ruth told me that Naomi felt that you, Lord God, had really made her life bitter, and so she wanted to be known by the name Marah, which means "bitter".'[55]

'A perfect answer,' the Lord God replies. 'Here is your final question. Why did Naomi and her family leave Bethlehem in the first place and move to Moab?'

Again Eve looks excited about this question. 'Ruth told me about that yesterday as well. The family had to move because there was a severe famine in the land.'[56]

'Excellent!' the Lord God says. 'Like Ruth, you have answered every one of your questions correctly.' The others give Eve a big round of applause.

Then the Lord God says to them all, 'As Eve and Ruth have answered all their questions correctly, there is no need to continue. Moses and Joshua have both answered some questions wrongly and therefore have no chance of winning. The two who will remain until tomorrow and can look forward to a fine meal are Eve and Ruth. The rest of you must go from the tent by sundown.'

Initially there is silence. The end seems to have come so quickly. Rahab is the first to make a move, and she goes over to Eve and Ruth and congratulates them.

'It's not as if there are any real winners or losers here,' says Moses. 'It has been an extremely interesting time, and I think we have learned a great deal from each other. Something tells me that we will meet again soon.'

Moses' words seem to break the ice. They all start talking at once, telling each other what an amazing few days it has been. Saul and David hug each other. Who would have thought on Day One that they would ever reach this point?

'I think Moses is quite right.' Eve surveys the group. 'There are no winners or losers here. What have Ruth and I won anyway? We'll simply be here for one more day, and then we too will have to leave.'

'I suppose, in one way we have all won,' Joshua adds. 'We have learned so much. Look at David and Saul, for example. If anybody's a winner it's got to be those two!'

A while later, the Lord God tells them that it is time for the five of them to head towards the gate. Ruth and Eve hug the others in farewell, the gate opens as it has done in the past, and Moses, Joshua, Rahab, Saul and David walk through into the light. They turn one last time and wave to Eve and Ruth. When the last one has gone through, the huge gate closes and, after a moment, Eve and

Ruth walk back in silence to the main tent. The two of them sit down at the table, still silent and deep in thought.

Eventually Ruth asks Eve, 'Where do you think they have gone?'

'I don't really know, but Moses said something that made me think. He said we would probably all see each other again. There is something special about that light beyond the gate!'

'I've been thinking that as well,' says Ruth. 'I think the Lord God dwells in that light. I think it's a place of real happiness and peace. I'm beginning to feel as if I have lost instead of winning, being left behind here.'

'I feel exactly the same,' Eve replies.

'You will both soon find out the answers to your questions,' says the Lord God. 'Now, you should wash and ready yourselves for the meal that I shall prepare for you.'

Eve and Ruth do as they are told. When they return to the main table in the living area, the Lord God has indeed made a wonderful meal for them. There is fine wine, venison, a variety of cooked vegetables and fresh fruit. They sit at the table and together say a blessing for the food.

As they eat, Ruth asks Eve to explain a little more about how it was in the beginning, in Paradise.

'I don't think I can ever put it into words, Ruth,' Eve replies. 'It is such a distant memory, but I do know that it is a place I long to return to.'

'I think it's a place where we all long to be,' says Ruth softly.

Eve continues, 'I think we were made to live for ever somewhere. In a real sense I think we were made for heaven, for Paradise,[57] which is the dwelling place of the Lord God. I truly believe that that is where we shall be returning when we walk through the gate into the light.'

'Is that where the Lord God's throne is, and all his angels?'

'I believe it is.'

'I wonder where heaven is,' Ruth says, half to herself.

'I don't think anyone could ever answer that,' Eve replies.

They sit for a while in silence, pondering these things.

Ruth speaks again. 'Although I don't know where heaven is, in some strange way I have never felt far from heaven or from God's angels. I've also felt that I have not been far away from any loved ones of mine who have died, and I have certainly never felt very far from God. Eve, you were once in Paradise. What is heaven actually like?'

'Because I disobeyed the Lord God in the beginning, I'm afraid my memory of the garden, or heaven as it was, is now very vague,' Eve replies. 'I would certainly describe heaven as truly God's dwelling place.'[58]

'I've heard it's like a wonderful city designed and built by God,' adds Ruth.[59] 'A better place or country compared to anything we have ever known.[60] I wonder what we will do in heaven, when we go beyond that gate, if it is heaven we will be entering.'

Eve stands up from the table. 'It's so difficult to put this into words, Ruth. The vague memories I have of Paradise tell me that heaven is amazing. It will be a place where we can worship without distraction, serve without exhaustion, fellowship without fear, learn without fatigue, rest without boredom.'[61]

'They may only be words,' says Ruth, 'but that was beautiful.'

Now that they have finished their meal, Eve suggests they go for a walk and talk a little further. Before they do so, they both give thanks to the Lord God for a fine meal, and then they stroll outside. It's an exceptionally beautiful evening. The sun looks quite magnificent as it begins its final descent in the western skies.

Ruth looks at Eve. 'Do you think we will still know each other in heaven? Will I see Boaz again, and will you see Adam?'

Eve smiles. 'We will know each other in heaven, but in a different way. I like to think about how God actually knows us. He knows us completely, intimately, thoroughly, inside out. There is nothing hidden. When we get to heaven we'll know each other as God knows us, because all the imperfections of this life will be removed. In this life our sin causes us to cover ourselves, not just physically but also emotionally and spiritually.'

'In that sense,' says Ruth, 'in heaven we will know every person and they will all be friends and loved ones to us. We will know each other intimately.'[62]

'I know that when we enter heaven, Ruth, you will be able to pick your husband Boaz out of a crowd of millions of people,' Eve continues. You'll go up to him, hug him and say, "My darling. I knew it was you." Again, the joy you will experience cannot be put into words.'

At this point they hear the Lord God. 'Ruth and Eve, you have done so well. But you were right to say earlier that there are no winners or losers. The one way you have both been winners, however, is in your talk of what lies beyond the main gate. Throughout your lives you have never been far from what lies there. Yes, it is the Paradise of which you speak.'

Eve and Ruth clasp hands in sudden excitement. The Lord God goes on, 'I enjoyed listening to you talking about what you believe heaven is like. Eve is right. All you can use are mere words, but what you said is true. Now, you are going to experience something far beyond words. The joy you spoke of, the peace and happiness that lie beyond that gate, is something far more amazing than your minds can ever comprehend. You need not discuss it any more. It is time for you to pass through the gate and take your place in Paradise.'

Eve and Ruth are speechless. The whole meaning and point of their existence seems to focus on this moment in time. The huge gate ahead slowly opens. That same beautiful bright light begins to shine through. Eve and Ruth, still holding hands and trembling, although not with fear, start walking towards the gate. Simultaneously, they take one last look back at the tent, glance at each other and then pass through into the light.

Immediately, on the other side of the gate are Samson, Deborah and all the others who have been with them for the week. Ruth and Eve suddenly realize how intimately they know them all. All memory of old sin has gone—Samson and his many mistakes, the enmity of Saul and David. Any feeling of judging others has disappeared. Evil and sin are no more. They see how they are made in the image of God, and everything negative has gone, leaving only that reflection of God which is part of us all. It is so, so beautiful. Beyond, they see a vast crowd of people awaiting them. From this crowd, two shining figures approach Ruth and Eve. They are Adam and Boaz. They hold their wives in a heavenly embrace.

Adam looks at Eve, Boaz looks at Ruth. Both men speak at the same time: 'Welcome to Paradise, my darling.'

NOTES

1   Genesis 3:21

2   Exodus 4:17

3   1 Samuel 17

4   Judges 14:12–14; 16:7–14

5   Joshua 2

6   Read Judges 14—16. He kills a lion, captures 300 foxes, sets light to their tails and burns the Philistines' crops, and sleeps with a prostitute at Gaza.

7   Judges 4—5

8   1 Samuel 8—10

9   Having all this meat will be a great luxury for them. Meat would normally have been eaten only on special occasions, or when there had been a very successful hunt.

10   The Holy of Holies was the most sacred place inside the temple. It was only once a year, on the Day of Atonement, that the high priest was allowed to enter the Holy of Holies and offer a sacrifice for himself and for the sins of the people of Israel.

11   Judges 14:5–9

12   2 Samuel 11

13   For example, see Matthew 25:8

14   Hands were always washed under running water before meals, because there was no cutlery. Elisha used to pour water over the hands of Elijah, as his servant (2 Kings 3:11).

15   If Bathsheba was typical, bathing took place at the end of the day (2 Samuel 11:2).

16   It seems to have been customary to have two basic meals a day. In Luke 14:12, Jesus says, 'When you give a lunch or a dinner...'

17   See 1 Samuel 24:4

18   1 Samuel 24:2ff.

19   1 Samuel 26

20 1 Samuel 31:4
21 1 Samuel 18:7
22 1 Samuel 18:17–30
23 1 Samuel 24 and 26
24 A Nazarite was a person who showed their devotion to God by taking vows not to touch any alcohol (wine or beer), not to cut their hair, and not to touch dead bodies.
25 Judges 14—16
26 Romans 3:23
27 Psalm 67
28 Ruth 1:16–17
29 2 Samuel 11:2
30 2 Samuel 11—12
31 Exodus 34:29–35
32 Exodus 7:14—12:32
33 Joshua 3
34 Judges 15:16
35 1 Samuel 17
36 Genesis 9:21
37 Judges 4
38 Hebrews 11:29–31
39 Numbers 20:1–8
40 Numbers 20:9–12
41 1 Samuel 11
42 Psalm 150
43 Parts of Psalm 51
44 1 Samuel 15
45 1 Samuel 22
46 Joshua 2:8–11
47 Psalm 47
48 133 metres long, 22 metres wide and 13 metres high (Genesis 6:15)
49 Judges 4:12–16; 5:21
50 Judges 15:4–5

51 Exodus 20

52 1 Samuel 28:8–25; 31:1–6

53 2 Samuel 12:24–25. Jedidiah in Hebrew means 'Beloved of the Lord'.

54 1 Samuel 16:6–7

55 Ruth 1:20

56 Ruth 1:1, 6

57 '"Do not be worried and upset," Jesus told them. "Believe in God and believe also in me. There are many rooms in my Father's house, and I am going to prepare a place for you. I would not tell you this if it were not so. And after I go and prepare a place for you, I will come back and take you to myself, so that you will be where I am"' (John 14:1–3).

58 Psalm 33:13

59 Hebrews 11:10

60 Hebrews 11:16

61 Words from a sermon by David Burns, Minister of the Homer Church of Christ, called 'Heaven is a wonderful place', 25 February, 1996. (Source: Internet)

62 Peter, James and John recognized Moses and Elijah, even though they had been dead for hundreds of years, on the Mount of Transfiguration (Matthew 17:1–9).

THE BIBLE IN COCKNEY

Well, bits of it anyway

'Would you Adam and Eve it?' This was the headline of many of the national newspapers. The Holy Bible (well, bits of it anyway) has been translated into Cockney rhyming slang. Read how Jesus feeds five thousand geezers with just five loaves of Uncle Fred and two Lilian Gish. Or how Noah built a bloomin' massive nanny. Then there's always the story of David and that massive geezer Goliath, or the time when Simon's finger and thumb-in-law was Tom and Dick in Uncle Ned and Jesus healed her.

Mike's aim is for people to enjoy reading the Bible stories in this very down-to-earth version, and to help God's word reach out to those who wouldn't normally read the Bible but who may pick up a copy of this book.

ISBN 1 84101 217 3   £5.99
Available from your local Christian bookshop or direct from BRF using the order form on page 125.

MORE BIBLE IN COCKNEY

Prophets, proverbs and pioneers

'A pork pie has a short fork and knife, but the truth lives on forever, innit?' This book has a butcher's at some of the proverbs and psalms as well as the Ding Dong of Ding Dongs (Song of Songs). We'll find out about some of those great Old Testament prophets who got in a right old two-and-eight 'cos of the way the Israelites worshipped dodgy idols. There's Isaiah, and Jeremiah—that bloke who has a real hard lemon-and-lime of it—and then there's the story of Ezekiel and the Valley of the Dry Sticks and Stones.

To finish off, we have a complete translation of the Captain Hook of Acts into Cockney. Read how Jesus' early followers spread the good news about 'im and find out how Christianity really started. It began among the Jewish people, but then you'll see how it became a faith for the whole world.

ISBN 1 84101 259 9   £6.99
Available from your local Christian bookshop or direct from BRF using the order form on page 125.

★ Also by Mike Coles ★

Mike Coles interviews some biblical celebrity guests
in front of a live audience in the chat show...

SO YOU THINK YOU'RE A
NEW TESTAMENT WRITER

In an exclusive series of interviews, your host Mike Coles brings you
five encounters with the men who shaped the New Testament. This
is your chance to meet Matthew, Mark, Luke and John, as well as
Paul. Discover what motivated them and their writings, and find
out more about the consequences of their life-changing encounters
with Jesus Christ. The live—and lively—studio audience add a
whole lot of questions and comment.

Is Paul's anti-women reputation deserved? Can we trust a
reformed tax collector to tell the truth? What's the amazing new
'revelation' that John claims to have had on his island of exile? And
where can you get hold of the best wine, olive oil, or donkeys, in
town? In *So You Think You're a New Testament Writer* you'll find
answers to these questions!

ISBN 1 84101 183 5   £6.99
Available from your local Christian bookshop or direct from BRF using the
order form on page 125.

TO HAVE AND TO HOLD

Bible stories of love, loss and restoration

Anne Jordan Hoad

These imaginative retellings of Bible stories, some familiar, some less well-known, bring to life characters who, like so many of us, struggle in their personal relationships. It is easy to idealize such characters, assuming that they were somehow superior to mere human beings—and in idealizing them, we miss out on the lessons we can learn from their all-too-familiar experiences. Like us, they had to confront complex choices, survive difficult circumstances, wrestle with jealousy, dishonesty and pride. In hearing their stories again, we can identify and share in their fears and hopes, their sorrows and joys.

ISBN 1 84101 036 7   £6.99
Available from your local Christian bookshop or direct from BRF using the order form on page 125.

BIBLE VOICES

Meditations from creation to apocalypse

Anthony Geering

The Bible is rich in wonderful stories, powerful characters, and themes of love, life and death. This collection of monologues acts as an introduction to these stories for those scared off by the idea of a 'holy book', as well as encouraging others to look again at familiar passages and ideas. Written with insight, challenge and humour, they bring to vivid life the people and events of the Bible, both great and small.

Some may enjoy reading them alone as meditations, or sharing them with a group for discussion. But this book is chiefly designed to provide ideal material for inspiring presentations for church services, school assemblies or even after-dinner speeches!

ISBN 1 84101 145 2   £6.99
Available from your local Christian bookshop or direct from BRF using the order form on page 125

DREAM STORIES

A journey into the Bible's dreams and visions

Russ Parker

Dreams have fascinated humanity for thousands of years. In today's sceptical culture, we tend to dismiss dreams as having little or no importance, yet almost everybody has at least one dream they remember which may have had an effect upon them, sometimes lasting for many years.

In the Bible, dreams and visions were seen as powerful ways in which God communicated with his people. Prophets, early leaders of the Christian Church, and rulers of foreign powers experienced dreams that had impact and consequence for the dreamer and those about him.

Dream Stories takes a look at how God spoke to his people through their dreams, from Jacob's dream at Bethel to Paul's night-time vision calling him to Macedonia. Russ Parker draws on 20 years' experience of pastoral ministry and examines these stories, showing how God still speaks to us through our dreams, bringing fresh opportunities for healing and growth.

ISBN 1 84101 072 3   £6.99

Available from your local Christian bookshop or direct from BRF using the order form on page 125.

THE SCEPTIC'S GUIDE TO
READING THE BIBLE

A 'no-strings' exploration for those
who have given up or never really tried

Hilary Brand

Many people believe in God and respect the teachings of Jesus and yet find it almost impossible to read the Bible for themselves. It's too ancient; it's too difficult; it carries too much institutional baggage and, above all, it leaves more questions than answers. It's not surprising that apathy sets in!

This book aims to throw away the religious rule-book, scrape away preconceptions and offer a 'no strings' approach to reading the Bible. It suggests different approaches to the Bible's varied types of literature and offers a range of techniques for Bible reading, ranging from the imaginative to the analytical and from the broad sweep to the tiny phrase. It looks unflinchingly at the Bible's hard questions and gathers comments from many famous and influential people on what the Bible means to them.

In short, this book aims to make reading the Bible accessible. It may well stimulate questions as well as answers, but both have the power to energize and transform.

ISBN 1 84101 084 7   £7.99
Available from your local Christian bookshop or direct from BRF using the order form on page 125.

REF	TITLE	PRICE	QTY	TOTAL
217 3	*The Bible in Cockney*	£5.99		
259 9	*More Bible in Cockney*	£6.99		
183 5	*So You Think You're a New Testament Writer*	£6.99		
036 7	*To Have and to Hold*	£6.99		
145 2	*Bible Voices*	£6.99		
072 3	*Dream Stories*	£6.99		
084 7	*The Sceptic's Guide to Reading the Bible*	£7.99		

POSTAGE AND PACKING CHARGES					
order value	UK	Europe	Surface	Air Mail	Postage and packing:
£7.00 & under	£1.25	£3.00	£3.50	£5.50	Donation:
£7.01–£30.00	£2.25	£5.50	£6.50	£10.00	Total enclosed:
Over £30.00	free	prices on request			

Name _____ Account Number _____

Address _____

_____ Postcode _____

Telephone Number _____ Email _____

Payment by: Cheque ❑ Mastercard ❑ Visa ❑ Postal Order ❑ Switch ❑

Credit card no. ❑❑❑❑ ❑❑❑❑ ❑❑❑❑ ❑❑❑❑ Expires ❑❑ ❑❑

Switch card no. ❑❑❑❑❑❑❑❑❑❑❑❑❑❑❑❑❑❑

Issue no. of Switch card ❑❑❑❑ Expires ❑❑ ❑❑

Signature _____ Date _____

All orders must be accompanied by the appropriate payment.

Please send your completed order form to:
BRF, First Floor, Elsfield Hall, 15–17 Elsfield Way, Oxford OX2 8FG
Tel. 01865 319700 / Fax. 01865 319701 Email: enquiries@brf.org.uk

❑ Please send me further information about BRF publications.

Available from your local Christian bookshop.   BRF is a Registered Charity

New Daylight, BRF's popular series of Bible reading notes, is ideal for those looking for a fresh, devotional approach to reading and understanding the Bible. Each issue covers four months of daily Bible reading and reflection with each day offering a Bible passage (text included), helpful comment and a prayer or thought for the day ahead.

New Daylight is written by a gifted team of contributors including Adrian Plass, Margaret Cundiff, David Winter, Gordon Giles, Rachel Boulding, Peter Graves, Helen Julian CSF, David Spriggs, Margaret Silf, Jenny Robertson and Veronica Zundel.

New Daylight is also available in large print and on cassette for the visually impaired.

NEW DAYLIGHT SUBSCRIPTIONS

❏ I would like to give a gift subscription
(please complete both name and address sections below)
❏ I would like to take out a subscription myself
(complete name and address details only once)

This completed coupon should be sent with appropriate payment to BRF. Alternatively, please write to us quoting your name, address, the subscription you would like for either yourself or a friend (with their name and address), the start date and credit card number, expiry date and signature if paying by credit card.

Gift subscription name _____

Gift subscription address _____

_____ Postcode _____

Please send to the above, beginning with the next January/May/September issue: (delete as applicable)

(please tick box)	UK	SURFACE	AIR MAIL
NEW DAYLIGHT	❏ £11.70	❏ £13.05	❏ £15.30
NEW DAYLIGHT 3-year sub	❏ £29.25		

Please complete the payment details below and send your coupon, with appropriate payment to: **BRF, First Floor, Elsfield Hall, 15–17 Elsfield Way, Oxford OX2 8FG**

Your name _____

Your address _____

_____ Postcode _____

Total enclosed £ _____ (cheques should be made payable to 'BRF')

Payment by cheque ❏ postal order ❏ Visa ❏ Mastercard ❏ Switch ❏

Card number: ⬚⬚⬚⬚⬚⬚⬚⬚⬚⬚⬚⬚⬚⬚⬚⬚⬚⬚⬚⬚

Expiry date of card: ⬚⬚⬚⬚ Issue number (Switch): ⬚⬚⬚⬚

Signature (essential if paying by credit/Switch card)_____

❏ Please do not send me further information about BRF publicaations.

NB: BRF notes are also available from your local Christian bookshop. **BRF is a Registered Charity**

brf

Resourcing your spiritual journey

through...

- Bible reading notes
- Books for Advent & Lent
- Books for Bible study and prayer
- Books to resource those working with under 11s in school, church and at home

- Quiet days and retreats
- Training for primary teachers and children's leaders
- Godly Play
- Barnabas Live

For more information, visit the **brf** website at **www.brf.org.uk**